# CURIOSITIES

## OF

# FOOTBALL

# CURIOSITIES
## —OF—
# FOOTBALL

## JONATHAN RICE

PAVILION

CARTOONS BY ROBERT DUNCAN

First published in Great Britain in 1996 by
PAVILION BOOKS LIMITED
26 Upper Ground, London SE1 9PD

Text copyright © 1996 by Jonathan Rice
Cartoons copyright © 1996 by Robert Duncan

A CIP catalogue record for this book is available from
the British Library

ISBN 1 85793 986 7

Typeset in Sabon
Designed by Nigel Partridge
Printed and bound in Finland by WSOY

2 4 6 8 10 9 7 5 3 1

This book may be ordered by post direct from the publisher.
Please contact the Marketing Department.
But try your bookshop first.

# CONTENTS

# INTRODUCTION

I cannot trace my interest in football back to a particular time or place. It is just that, being left-handed, I have always tended to read newspapers from back to front, so it was the sports pages that I noticed first. And the sports pages of British newspapers have always devoted more column inches to football than to any other sport. By that criterion, it is truly the national sport. Indeed, although the original rules of Association Football were drawn up in England, it did not take long for the game to spread overseas, and now it is the national sport of over a hundred different countries, a national obsession all over the world.

If I cannot say when I first became aware of football, I can date absolutely the moment when my interest in football became an obsession. It was 15 February 1958, nine days after the Munich air crash, and the place was Upton Park. My father had procured two tickets for the FA Cup fifth-round tie between West Ham United and Fulham, and as a birthday treat, I was to accompany him. I had no particular interest in either club before the game, but I asked my older brother which of the two he would support. He thought about it for a bit and then decided he preferred West Ham. I therefore resolved to support Fulham, then a Second Division club of no particular pretensions. I was just one of 37,500 people who packed the stadium that cold day, but by the end of the game I had undergone the sort of transformation that only eleven-year-olds can understand. I was no longer merely interested in football, I was devoted to the game, and to Fulham in particular. You see, they won 3–2. Goals from Roy Dwight (Elton John's cousin, who was to score and then break his leg in the Notts Forest/Luton Cup Final of 1959), Jimmy Hill and England's own Johnny Haynes more than cancelled two West Ham efforts from Mike Grice and John Bond, and I was in heaven. The pantheon of angels in my football heaven begins with the Fulham eleven that day: Macedo; Cohen, Langley; Bentley, Stapleton, Lawler; Dwight, Hill, Stevens, Haynes, Chamberlain.

Memory plays many tricks, and I have always thought that Fulham lost almost every other game they played from the moment I began supporting them. But a look at the record books shows this is not true. A week after that Cup tie, they beat Grimsby Town 6–0 in the League, and they went on to the semi-finals of the FA Cup, where they lost in the replay 5–3 to the post-Munich Manchester United, and I was one of the few people in the entire country hoping that Manchester United would lose (a sentiment that I have consistently upheld ever since). Had it not been for a run of only two points in five games in April, Fulham would have been promoted, a feat they achieved the next season, thanks to a run of six consecutive victories at the start of the 1958–9 season. It may be a curiosity of football to think of Fulham winning a few matches, but those were the glory days indeed. They lost the next time they played West Ham in the Cup, after their best days were over in 1963, and again the time after that, but that was the 1975 FA Cup Final at Wembley.

Supporting Fulham makes me the ideal candidate for writing a book on soccer's oddities, as a trip to Craven Cottage is never without incident. I remember the game against Cardiff City in December 1968, when I arrived five minutes late, just as a goal was thumping into the net. I turned to the man next to me on the terraces and said, 'Lucky I didn't miss the goal,' to which he replied, 'What do you mean? That makes it 2–1.' Fulham went on to lose 5–1. And what about the game against (I think) Manchester City on the day of the Boat Race one season before the Eric Miller Stand was built. As the two crews rowed past the ground, all the spectators on the river side turned to watch the Boat Race, rather than the ineffectual efforts of the twenty-two men on the pitch. No wonder that by the end of the 1980s one of the advertising hoardings at Craven Cottage read, 'Lonely? Depressed? Suicidal? Ring the Samaritans.' They must have done a roaring trade.

I have played, watched and written about football for years. I was my school's Under-14 team goalkeeper, and kept a clean sheet for an entire season, thanks largely to the fact that the two games fixed for the Under-14s that year were both cancelled due to adverse weather conditions. A couple of seasons later, I was in goal during a school inter-house game when we lost 26–0. I am only willing to take the blame for fifteen of the goals because: (a) I was taken out of goal once the score reached 16–0, and (b) one of those sixteen was an own goal by Miller, my right full back, who, when I suggested he pass back to me, turned and shot the ball with immense power high into the top corner of the net. Definitely his fault. What is more, I kept the score within the bounds of mental arithmetic and the referee's pencil by virtue of the fact that there were no nets in the goal, allowing me to take my time in retrieving the ball from distant parts after each goal had been thumped past me. I was half-hoping to be sent off for time-wasting after the twelfth goal caused me to scramble around in a bush halfway down a river bank for about five minutes, but the referee was probably unaware of his powers in that respect. When I finally hung up my boots, after years of playing for my school's old boys' fourth XI and for the Yokohama Country and Athletic Club, it was with much personal regret, but with the sighs of relief of my team-mates ringing in my ears.

Watching football is a continuing pleasure. I have seen Cup Finals, internationals and non-League matches in several continents. I remember Tottenham Hotspur versus All Japan at the National Stadium in Tokyo in the early 1970s, when the Spurs side, all hungover after a night out on the tiles, conceded a goal within five minutes and decided they had better play properly for a while. By half-time they were 5–1 up, and every player spent the second half desperately trying to catch his manager's attention so that he could be substituted. I have conga-ed with Brazilians down a Los Angeles hotel corridor after the 1994 World Cup Final, and I have suffered in the cold and the rain as Walsall drew with St Albans in the second round of the Cup in 1968–9. I have watched with barely 400 others as Forfar Athletic beat Arbroath in a pre-season friendly and I have even survived standing in the away fans enclosure at Loftus Road with eight ten-year-old QPR fans as Rangers beat Chelsea 6–0. Every goal was greeted with a stony silence from all at the Chelsea end, except for eight little boys who cheered wildly. I checked my life-insurance policy again that night.

*Curiosities of Football* follows *Cricket, Golf* and *Politics* in the same series. My thanks are due to all sorts of people for making this book possible. First, there is the late John Anstey at the *Daily Telegraph* magazine, who first commissioned me to write on football for money, and who allowed me to write something other than back-page copy. I must also thank Colin Webb and his team at Pavilion, for letting me develop the original *Curiosities* idea into what is now threatening to become a long-running series; and also my agent, Mark Lucas, for his efforts to develop the career of one of his few authors who has not spent much of his life chained to a radiator in the Middle East. Suppliers of curiosities have been many, but I should thank in particular Colin Morgan, whose library of 1940s football magazines has been a wonderful source of bizarre moments; Jim Kelly of the *Financial Times* and Andy Harris of Avalon Productions, who came up with a couple of very bizarre curiosities. Michael Parkinson has been more than usually supportive, by asking *Daily Telegraph* readers to supply me with footballing curiosities, which resulted in a postbag consisting of perhaps eighty odd events at Craven Cottage and four or five in all of the rest of the world! Still, several of them have found their way into this book. Most of all, I should thank my two very willing and extremely underpaid researchers, my sons Alex and Tom, who between them have come up with hundreds of curiosities in a remarkably short time, which I have tried to weave into something that resembles a book.

JONATHAN RICE
April 1996

# KICK-OFF

Kicking things is an inbred urge in the human psyche. Balls are good things to kick because, more often than not, they do not kick back. So football has a history that goes back many centuries and across many cultures. In most societies, ball games have always existed (or at least they have existed since the invention of the ball, whenever that was), and in most societies people used their feet as often as their hands. Football has probably the longest recordable ancestry of any team sport, even if what was being played in earlier centuries was not called football. The twelve-volume *Book of Football*, a great early work on football published in 1905, suggested that the game began when Cain and Abel kicked an apple around the Garden of Eden in 5000 BC, but there is little archaeological evidence for this claim. Indeed, as their parents Adam and Eve were banished from the Garden for picking apples before Cain and Abel were born, it all seems highly unlikely. Perhaps they had climbed over the fence to go scrumping for apples, the ones their Mum and Dad had said were so good, or else had kicked their ball over the next-door Garden wall, and had gone round to ask God to give it back. We know little else about the brothers, except that Cain killed Abel and got banished yet again, this time to the land of Nod. He seemed to spend his entire career getting red cards from the great Ref in the sky.

In China 500 years before the birth of Christ, they played *tsu chu*, which can be roughly translated as 'kicking a leather ball'; in ancient Greece they played *episkyros*, and in ancient Rome it was *harpastum*, both ball games played by two teams; a thousand years later, in the Japanese court in the Heian period, the court nobles played a more individual game of skill that involved keeping a ball in the air using only the feet. At about the same time, the Normans brought to England a game called *la soule*, which by the fourteenth century had developed into a free-for-all in the town centres with an inflated pig's bladder as a ball.

The governments of the day did not approve. In 1287, the Synod of Exeter banned 'wrestling, dancing and other unseemly sports' from its churchyards, one of the favourite unseemly sports being football. King Edward II's ministers, in 1314, issued a proclamation stating that 'Forasmuch as there is a great noise in the city caused by Hustling over large balls, from which many evils may arise, which God forbid, we command and forbid, on behalf of the King, on pain of imprisonment, such game to be used in the city in future.' It is impossible to tell how many footballers were imprisoned (a feature of footballing life that continues to this day), but in 1349, Edward II's son Edward III was forced to repeat the prohibition, describing football as one of many 'foolish games which are of no use'. Edward II's grandson Richard II and great-grandson Henry IV also issued decrees against football in 1389 and 1401. In 1531, Sir Thomas Elyot (1490–1546) wrote in his treatise *The Boke Named the Governour* that football was 'nothing but beastlie furie and extreme violence'. *The Boke Named The Governour* was a treatise on education: this is the first evidence in English, but by no means the last, that education and football are incompatible.

Queen Elizabeth I claimed, when addressing her troops at Tilbury in 1588, that she had 'the heart and stomach of a king, and of a king of England, too' and she proved this not only by spurring on her fighting men to victory over the Spanish Armada, but also by continuing the tradition of her male ancestors by banning football. 'No football play to be used or suffered within the City of London' was her decree of 1572, a law dutifully supported by the Puritan pamphleteer Philip Stubbes. Stubbes is remembered – if he is remembered at all – mainly for one work, *The Anatomie of Abuses*, published in 1583. This was an enthusiastic attack on all forms of social evil, from fashion and the theatre to football. Stubbes described football, probably very accurately, as more 'a bloody murthering practice than a fellowly sport or pastime'. He felt that it caused 'fighting, brawling, contention, quarrel picking, murder, homicide and great effusion of blood'. Things have not changed much in the subsequent 400 years.

Matters were, however, beginning to improve for the footballing community of Britain. In 1615, two centuries after his predecessor Henry IV had been the fourth English king to ban football, the first king of both England and Scotland, James I and VI respectively, attended a football match in Wiltshire. The final score has not been recorded for posterity, but then neither have the names of the two teams taking part, but the mere fact that royalty should attend a football match without banning it, either in advance or in retrospect, showed that football was beginning to be seen as a lawful part of British life. James I's grandson, Charles II, is also recorded as having attended a football match, in 1681, between a team of members of the Royal Household and a team of the Duke of Albemarle's servants. Christopher Monck, 2nd (and last) Duke of Albemarle, was a West Countryman, born in Devon and later becoming Lord Lieutenant of that county. His uncle Nicholas had been a clergyman in Cornwall. His servants (who may well have included soldiers of the Horse Guards, of whom he was also in command) were probably the driving force behind the fixture with the king's men, as at this time the main football-playing area of Britain seems to have been in the west. The king himself was known far more for his love of horse-racing and real tennis than of any kind of football.

15

The organized sport we now know as Association Football has its origin in the muscular Christianity of Victorian Britain. In 1801, the northern writer Joseph Strutt (1765–1844) had remarked that football was a very popular but nevertheless still a very vicious game, and 'when the exercise becomes exceedingly violent, the players kick each other's shins'. The great reformers of the middle and late nineteenth century, spurred on by their belief in the essential wickedness of man and in his perpetual need for correction, finally got round to the subject of kicking each other's shins, although different

groups of Christian reformers got there by quite separate routes. There were the city missions, mainly Church of England or Methodist, aimed at rescuing the poor town and city workers from their lives of squalid monotony; and there were the great public schools, with their deeply religious and often hair-shirted reverend headmasters, whose preoccupations seemed to be manly sports and the organization thereof. Both branches of the Church saw football as a healthy means of channelling aggression and teaching the important lessons of team spirit and competition. And football was cheap and simple to organize. All you needed was a fairly flat area of rough ground (although in Yeovil they have never quite understood the concept of 'fairly flat') and twenty-two players. It didn't even matter what the weather was like.

Thus it was that Aston Villa, for example, began as an offshoot of the local Wesleyan chapel. The Revd T.T. Preedy, curate at St Peter's Church, was the driving force behind the formation of Barnsley FC, and the Revd Gordon Young of St Jude's Church and the Droop Street Board School got Queen's

Park Rangers going. Wolverhampton Wanderers was formed at St Luke's Church School, Blakenhall, and the Revd K.R.G. Hunt was one of their best players in the early days. It was the Revd Pitt who organized football in Swindon, and Southampton FC is still known by the nickname 'The Saints' because of its formation out of the Young Men's Association of St Mary's, Southampton.

Not all clubs had such a holy start. Middlesbrough was founded in 1876 by a group of soccer enthusiasts at a tripe supper. Chelsea Football Club was founded in 1905 after a discussion in a local pub, showing that the link between alcohol and football is just as strong as the link between football and the Almighty. Almost a century later, the drink link is far stronger: many competitions and many more teams are sponsored by drinks companies, but few are sponsored by the Church. Still, more people go to church than attend football matches on a Sunday, although the gap is closing. Soon the only link between the two will be the singing of 'Abide With Me' at the Cup Final, and the fact that Pope John Paul II is season-ticket holder no. 108,000 at Barcelona FC.

The public schoolboys were busy forming clubs as well. In 1790 there had been reference to football at Winchester College, and in 1823 William Webb Ellis famously picked up the ball at Rugby College and ran with it, thus creating at a stroke the separate sport of rugby football. It seems likely that rugby football developed simply because football was played on grass at Rugby, whereas it was played on flagstones or cobblestones at many other public schools. Tackling an opponent by throwing yourself at his knees, or diving over the ball to prevent a try are not manoeuvres that should be tried on anything but a comparatively soft surface. It was quarter of a century after the invention of rugby football

17

before the parent game set about putting its house in order. The 'Cambridge Rules' of 1848 were drawn up at Cambridge University by old boys from Eton, Harrow, Shrewsbury and Winchester, to try to give some organizational framework to what was apparently little more than a milling throng fighting over a pig's bladder. The new rules seemed to work, by and large, and fourteen years later, in 1862, a certain Mr J.C. Thring of Uppingham College drafted a set of ten rules for what he described as 'the simplest game'. In November that year, a game was played between Old Etonians and Old Harrovians at Cambridge, and the rules passed their first strict test. But the rules were not very detailed. Although there was enough order in the world of football for the Football Association to be formed in 1863, the size of the ball, for example, was not settled until 1872, ten years after Mr Thring's rules had been drawn up.

From then on, things moved very quickly. The establishment of the Football Association occurred after a meeting in a tavern in central London, and set itself the immediate task of establishing 'a definite code of rules'. Among the twelve founder-members was the Blackheath club, which played its football by the rugby code, so this presented an unusual challenge to the ingenuity of the other eleven, which all disapproved of the hacking, body-tackling and handling the ball that were the accepted norm in rugby football. After six meetings at which they all tried to find a compromise, they admitted defeat and Blackheath left the Football Association. Eight years later, they became founder-members of the Rugby Union, the only club to be founder-members of the governing bodies of both sports.

In the last three decades of the nineteenth century there were two major developments that led to the establishment

of football as the leading international sport of the past one hundred years. One of these developments was not, in fact, the first record of a member of the royal family actually playing football rather than merely watching it (HRH Prince Albert, Prince of Wales, later King Edward VII, played full back in a Royal Household game against a House of Commons XI), although royal patronage has never hindered the development of any sport. The first of these events was the establishment of the Football Association Cup, proposed in 1871 and first staged the following winter. The competition got off to a patchy start, with only fifteen clubs entering, three of which scratched before their first game. All the teams but two were from the south and east of England, not at that time – or now – the real stronghold of football. The two exceptions were Queen's Park of Glasgow, which became the first of eight Scottish clubs to have competed in the English FA Cup competition, and Donington Grammar School, from Spalding in Lincolnshire. These two teams were due to meet in the first round of the first competition, but could not arrange a suitable date, so both teams advanced to the second round, where they were due to meet again. This time Donington Grammar School scratched from the competition and never entered it again.

Those first fifteen clubs taking part in the FA Cup competition did not have the benefit of a referee's whistle (first used in 1876) or goal nets (invented by a Mr Brodie of Liverpool and not used in the FA Cup until 1891–2). Thus it came as no particular surprise that the first competition was a little chaotic. The Wanderers, the eventual winners of the trophy, were a public-school side that developed out of the Forest club of London, formed in 1859. The club disbanded in 1882, but in the first nine years of the competition they won the Cup five times, and were only ever beaten by Oxford University (twice) and Old Etonians (twice). Their players included Charles Alcock, the second secretary of the Football Association and also secretary of Surrey County Cricket Club, whose headquarters was (and still is) the Kennington Oval, where all but one of the first twenty Cup Finals were held. Alcock captained the Wanderers to their first success in that first competition, a clear case of 'It's my ball, so I'm going to win.' Less successful than the Wanderers were Harrow Chequers, a team of Harrow old boys, which scratched from the competition before their first match, and repeated this odd feat in 1874–5 and 1875–6. Although their home ground was the Kennington Oval, they never entered the FA Cup again after 1876, and thus were unable to claim the all-time record of being the first club to play a home cup tie on that year's Cup Final ground. The only club ever to have played a home tie on the ground chosen for that season's Cup Final – not counting replays – is Chelsea, whose Stamford Bridge ground was used for three finals between 1920 and 1922. In 1920,

Chelsea even reached the semi-final round, beating Swindon Town, Leicester City and Bradford at Stamford Bridge on the way, and had they won through to the final, the venue would have had to be switched, as competition rules state that the final must be played on a neutral ground. But Aston Villa beat them 3–1 in the semi-final at Bramall Lane, and the FA were not put to the bother of having to find an alternative ground at the last minute.

The remaining eleven clubs in that first FA Cup competition were Upton Park (not connected with the present West Ham United, they were an amateur club who represented Britain in the 1900 Olympics and won the gold medal); Clapham Rovers (Cup winners in 1880); Crystal Palace (no relation of the present League club); Hitchin Town (which played in the first round proper over more than a 100-year span by reaching the main stages four times in the 1970s); Maidenhead (which reached the first round proper in 1971–2, exactly one hundred years after the first competition); Marlow (the only club to have competed in every FA Cup since its inception – in 1881–2 they reached the semi-finals); the Royal Engineers (two captains and nine lieutenants, they were the strong favourites but lost in the final); Reigate Priory (founded in the same year they first entered the FA Cup and which in 1996 celebrated 125 years of playing on the same ground); Hampstead Heathens (which reached the third round, but never entered the FA Cup again); Barnes (the only club ever beaten by the Hampstead Heathens, they were formed by Ebenezer Cobb Morley, the first secretary of the FA); and the Civil Service (which competed in the first five FA Cups, but never had a home tie and never won a game).

The first FA Cup Final was held at Kennington Oval on 16 March 1872. It included the first injury, when Lt Edmund W.

Creswell, one of the Royal Engineers' forwards, fell and broke his collar-bone after only ten minutes. He played on, but his team was unable to prevent the Wanderers scoring the only goal of the game five minutes later. The goal was credited to 'A.H. Chequer', but this was actually a pseudonym for one Morton Peto Betts. It seems likely that because Betts was a member of the Harrow Chequers team that had scratched from the competition without playing a game, the official scorers felt that a chap should not play for two teams in the same competition, and thus credited the goal to 'a Harrow Chequer'. His captain in the final was, as we have seen, the secretary of the Football Association, who did not seem to have the same scruples; anyway, in those amateur days there were no regulations about transferring from club to club.

Alcock's idea of a knockout competition was one of the two great footballing projects of the late Victorian era. The FA Cup was essentially an amateur project, but the other was a professional concept – the formation of the Football League, in 1888. The first meeting of the body that would turn itself into the Football League took place at Anderton's Hotel in

London on 22 March that year. It is a mild curiosity that the meeting took place in London, because the original impetus behind the development of the League came entirely from the north, in particular from Lancashire. In an age when there was no professional sport in England, it was often remarked that Scottish footballers seemed to have arrived in Lancashire in mysterious circumstances, and then 'missed the train back', as the official League history published in 1938 put it. 'The influx of so many Scotsmen under suspicious circumstances led to a crisis which had far-reaching consequences.' As usual, it was foreigners who were to blame. In 1888, there were still no professional clubs south of Birmingham.

Professional footballers had to have games in which to play. In the 1870s, games started late, or not at all, or at the wrong ground, and it was obvious that football would never develop properly, or, more importantly, ever make money unless somebody organized it. Luckily, England at that time was swarming with organizers. The League began in the autumn of 1888 with twelve clubs, none of which had played in the original FA Cup competition only seventeen years earlier. They were six Lancashire clubs (Accrington Stanley, Blackburn Rovers, Bolton Wanderers, Burnley, Everton and Preston North End) and six from the Midlands (Aston Villa, Derby County, Notts County, Stoke, West Bromwich Albion and Wolverhampton Wanderers).

The League began its first games before the points system had been decided. It kicked off on 8 September 1888, with just 5 games (Bolton Wanderers 3, Derby County 6; Everton 2, Accrington Stanley 1; Preston North End 5, Burnley 2; Stoke 0, West Bromwich Albion 2; Wolverhampton Wanderers 1, Aston Villa 1). Blackburn Rovers and Notts County played their first games a week later: Blackburn began with a 5–5 draw against Accrington Stanley at home, followed by a 6–2 win against West Bromwich Albion, who were the leading proponents of a points system that ignored everything except wins. It was not until 21 November 1888 (by which time West Brom had won six of the first eleven matches of the season) that the long-lasting system of two points for a win and one for a draw was agreed. Even if no points had been awarded for a drawn game, it would have made no difference to the destination of the League title in that first season. Preston North End won eighteen of their twenty-two games, and nobody else won more than twelve. There were not that many drawn games anyway. With an average of 4.5 goals per game, disciplined defence was a concept whose time was still well in the future. It was not until Burnley won the Second Division title in 1897–8, despite winning one fewer game than the runners-up Newcastle United, that the points for a draw played a part in deciding a divisional title. Nobody won the First Division title without being the most winning team of the season until 1920–1. Then, by a curious coincidence, it was Burnley again. They took the title by five points from Manchester City despite winning one game fewer.

The League spread professionalism across the country, but it would still be another five years before a London club joined the Football League. Arsenal came into the Second Division for the 1893–4 season, but was the only club south of the Birmingham area in the League until Luton Town joined in 1897–8, only to lose their place to Stockport County after just three seasons. Bristol City were the third southern club to achieve League status, in 1901–2, and in 1904, Arsenal became the first southern team to reach the First Division. Tottenham Hotspur had won the FA Cup as a non-League side in 1901, but Arsenal's climb to the top division of the

Football League marked the final spread of professional football southwards. Within a few seasons, Chelsea, Leyton Orient, Fulham and Tottenham were in the League, Spurs equalling Bury and Glossop North End's record of being promoted after their first season in the League.

Getting into the League was not easy for Spurs. In 1896 they were one of ten clubs that applied for one of the three places available, but they were beaten by Blackpool, Gainsborough Trinity and Walsall, not to mention Port Vale, Luton Town, Crewe Alexandra, Fairfield, Glossop North End and Macclesfield. For the next twelve years they played in the Southern League, but when Fulham were elected to the Football League from the Southern League in 1907, they decided to have another go at joining what was by then seen as the senior League competition. They made their intentions known early enough for the Southern League to insist on their resignation before the Football League met to decide on who should be asked to join for the next season. When it did meet, Lincoln City were not re-elected, but Bradford (Park Avenue) took their place. Spurs were not elected, so they were left without a competition to play in during the next season. Then Stoke resigned from the Football League through lack of support (a problem that does not seem to be a resignation matter these days), and another vacancy arose. A special meeting was called in June 1908, at which three clubs stood for the one vacancy. They were Spurs, Lincoln City (which had just lost their place a few weeks earlier) and, confusingly, Stoke, whose support had obviously reappeared overnight. On the first ballot, the voting was Lincoln City 17, Tottenham Hotspur 17 and Stoke 6. On a second ballot, with Stoke eliminated, the voting was Lincoln 20, Spurs 20. It went to the Management Committee, which voted 5 to 3 in favour of

Spurs. By the narrowest of margins ever recorded, they made it into the League. Lincoln City reappeared the next season.

By this time, organized football was truly up and running. There were paid referees with whistles, linesmen, goal nets, floodlights (candle power was tried in Sheffield in 1888: it almost worked) and a workable off-side law. There were international matches, penalty kicks (introduced in 1891) and away strips for League teams. There were points deducted for playing an ineligible player. There was Manchester United and Liverpool. There was massive national interest. It was time for things to go from being new and strange to being just plain strange.

### EXTRA TIME
*League clubs known by animal nicknames*
Lambs – Notts County
Lions – Millwall
Rams – Derby County
Spiders – Queen's Park, Glasgow
Stags – Mansfield Town

Tigers – Hull City
Wasps – Alloa
Wolves – Wolverhampton Wanderers

*League clubs known by bird nicknames*
Bantams – Coventry City
Bluebirds – Cardiff City
Canaries – Norwich City
Loons – Forfar Athletic
Magpies – Newcastle United
Owls – Sheffield Wednesday
Peacocks – Leeds United
Robins – Bristol City, Swindon Town
Seagulls – Brighton and Hove Albion
Swans – Swansea City
Throstles – West Bromwich Albion

*League clubs known by occupational nicknames*
Biscuitmen – Reading
Brewers – Watford
Chairboys – Wycombe Wanderers
Cobblers – Northampton Town
Fishermen – Grimsby Town
Foresters – Nottingham Forest
Glaziers – Crystal Palace
Gunners – Arsenal
Hatters – Luton Town, Stockport County
Merry Millers – Rotherham United
Pensioners – Chelsea
Potters – Stoke City
Railwaymen – Crewe Alexandra, Swindon Town
Saddlers – Walsall
Shrimpers – Southend United
Soldiers – Aldershot

*League clubs known by unimaginative nicknames*
B's – Brentford
O's – Leyton Orient
R's – Queen's Park Rangers
Blues – Birmingham City, Stranraer
Dark Blues – Dundee
Reds – Manchester United, Workington Town

*League clubs known by bizarre nicknames*
Bully Wee – Clyde
Gable Endies – Montrose
Grecians – Exeter City
Haddicks – Charlton Athletic
Lilywhites – Preston North End, Fulham
Moonrakers – Swindon Town
Red Lichties – Arbroath
Sandgrounders – Southport
Wee Rovers – Albion Rovers

*Football clubs named after days of the week*
Sheffield Wednesday (FA Premiership)
Abergavenny Thursdays (Abacus Welsh Football League)

*English Football League clubs have been known by the following club names*
City (16), United (16), Town (13), Athletic (5), County (4), Rovers (4), Wanderers (3), Albion (2), North End (2), Swifts (2), Alexandra (1), Argyle (1), Celtic (1), Forest (1), Hotspur (1), Ironopolis (1), Orient (1), Rangers (1), Stanley (1), Trinity (1), Victoria (1), Wednesday (1)

*Scottish clubs that have competed in the English FA Cup*
Cowlairs, 1886–7 (lost to Glasgow Rangers 3–2 in 3rd round)
Glasgow Rangers, 1885–6 (scratched) and 1886–7 (lost 3–1 to Aston Villa in the semi-final)
Gretna, 1993–4 (lost 3–2 to Blackpool in 1st round)
Heart of Midlothian, 1885–6 (scratched) and 1886–7 (lost 7-1 to Darwen in 1st round)
Partick Thistle, 1885–6 (lost 5–1 to Queen's Park in 1st round) and 1886–7 (lost 1–0 to Old Westminsters in 5th round)
Queen's Park, Glasgow (12 times between 1871–2 and 1886–7, beaten by Blackburn Rovers in the finals of 1883–4 and 1884–5)
Renton, 1886–7 (lost 2–0 to PNE in 3rd round)
Third Lanark, 1885–6 (scratched) and 1886–7 (lost 3–2 to Bolton W. in 2nd round)

*Irish clubs that have competed in the English FA Cup*
Belfast Distillery, 1887–8 (lost to Witton 4–2 in 2nd round) and 1889–90 (lost 10–2 to Bolton W. in 1st round)
Cliftonville, 1886–7 (lost 11–0 to Partick Thistle in 3rd round) and 1887–8 (scratched)

Linfield Athletic, 1888–9 (scratched in replay against Nottingham Forest, 1st round). Despite losing without a fight in the 1st round proper, Linfield scored 19 goals and conceded 8 in two qualifying rounds and the drawn first game against Notts Forest.

*Clubs that failed to be elected to the Football League include* Argonauts (1928), Ashton North End (1899), Fairfield (1895, 1896 and 1897), Folkestone (1934, 1935 and 1936), Halliwell (1888), Kettering (1900, 1927), Llanelli (1922), Mitchell St George's (1889), Newcastle East End (1892), Prescot Cables (1929, 1930), South Shore (1889), Sunderland Albion (1889 and 1891), West Stanley (1921)

# IT'S ALL ABOUT PLAYERS, REALLY

## 2

What makes a person want to become a footballer? Is it the primeval thrill of kicking a round leather object? Is it the physical satisfaction of proving one's fitness and co-ordination to one's peers? Is it because the sports teacher told you to play out on the wing and I don't care if it is cold and you have a sick note, you stay out on the wing until I blow the final whistle? Whatever the reasons – and they are as many as the number of managers who give 'all credit to the lad' in each television interview – the people who end up playing football seem to represent the oddest strands of society. Whether it is the chicken that follows the egg, or vice versa, is a subject for a greater sociological treatise than this. Do odd people play football because that is a game in which they can express themselves, or is football a curious game because of the people who play it?

If you want to be a footballer, you have to believe in yourself. It is no good imitating Maurice Cook, the Fulham forward of the late 1950s and early 1960s, who once asked his manager Frank Osborne for a transfer because he felt he was not good enough to play in the same team as Johnny Haynes. The Fulham fans (and there were some then) used to shout, 'Don't give it to Cookie' whenever Haynes had the ball at his feet. It also helps to have a powerful shot. Trevor Chamberlain, also of Fulham and for many seasons a regu-

lar alongside Cook and Haynes, was reputed to have broken a goalkeeper's arm with a penalty kick when he was still a schoolboy, and Jock McNabb, a Fulham player of the 1920s, once took a penalty that broke the net-retaining bar. Lindy Delapenha, the Jamaican Middlesbrough favourite of the early 1950s, once hit a penalty so hard that it went through the back of the net. This was in a match against Sunderland and one of the very first to be played under floodlights at Ayresome Park, so it was only understandable that the referee should be confused. He decreed that it was not a goal, and that the ball had gone into the goal under the side netting, which is a fantastic achievement from the penalty spot.

It also helps if you can decide in which position you like to play. Do not be like Tony Read, who was bought by Luton Town from Peterborough United in May 1964 as a goalkeeper. He played about 200 games for Luton over the next six years, but among those 200 appearances were twenty-eight as a forward. He even scored twelve goals, but never reached representative level, probably because nobody knew if he was going to play up front or between the posts until the game began. However, even Read could not compare with Adrian

Williams, who wore the no. 10 shirt for Reading against Wrexham on 5 March 1994, which meant that in only 130 games for the club and at the age of just twenty-two, he had played in every position, including once deputizing for an injured goalkeeper in 1992. Disappointingly, the following season he was only picked as a no. 5. Eric Tait, Berwick Rangers' longest-serving player, with 435 League appearances between 1970 and 1987 to his credit, played in every position for the club, and also ended up as player-manager. In August 1986, in a Skol Cup game at Albion Rovers, he picked himself as substitute, came on in the fifty-eighth minute, was booked in the fifty-ninth and sent off in the sixtieth without ever touching the ball. Berwick lost 3–1, so the crowd of 340 that packed into the Albion Rovers stadium went home happy.

In the 1940s, Piero Magni of Brescia played for his club in every position at least once, including one game as official goalkeeper. When Salvatore Giunta of Brescia was handed the no. 6 shirt on 14 April 1995 in the match against Roma, he had been picked in every position except goalkeeper, but admitted that he would never be likely to equal Magni's achievement, because 'a goalkeeper needs to know a lot, and I just don't possess that ability'. Most football fans would agree that goalkeepers have ability, but whether they know a lot is a different matter.

As Bobby Ferguson, West Ham's Scottish international goalkeeper once sagely remarked, 'It's all about players, really.' But if ordinary players are odd, goalkeepers are bizarre. Consider the case of Shane Kehoe, normally a centre back for Taghmon, an Irish team that plays in the Wexford League. A selection crisis resulted in Shane being asked to play in goal in the game against Tombruck United in March 1996, and chaos ensued. Tombruck needed to win to clinch the League

title, but they had not expected help from the opposing goal-keeper. Wearing a Liverpool FC baseball cap he had borrowed from a friend, Kehoe began the game as though goalkeeping was what he had done all his life. Then Tombruck attacked and a shot whistled towards him. He dived for the ball, grasped it cleanly in both hands and brought off a marvellous save. Unfortunately, in the process, his borrowed cap fell off and the wind blew it into the net. Before his team-mates had stopped admiring the way he had prevented a certain goal, and before he thought about kicking the ball upfield, Shane turned round to pick his cap out of the netting. Just a split second too late he realized that he was still holding the ball in his hands, and the referee had no hesitation in awarding a goal to Tombruck. Taghmon eventually went down 2–0 and Kehoe was substituted well before the final whistle. His team-mates were less than generous towards a man who was always quite sane when not wearing the goalie's jersey, and by pop-ular acclaim Kehoe's brief goalkeeping career was over. The popular acclaim came from his team and from the team who were overtaken by Tombruck and thus denied a chance of the

League championship thanks to Kehoe's absent-mindedness, but we must assume that Tombruck United's strikers would love to come up against that level of eccentricity in every goal-keeper they play against.

And they probably do. René Higuita's astonishing and tactically lunatic 'scorpion kick' at Wembley came over a century after the playing days of Bob Roberts, West Bromwich Albion's goalie, who had so little to do on 13 February 1886 while his team were beating Old Westminsters 6–0 in the sixth round of that year's FA Cup, that he engaged in snowball fights with spectators to keep himself warm. Higuita himself is known in Colombia as 'El Loco'. Given the amount of competition for the title in that country and among goalkeepers worldwide, it says a great deal for his eccentricity. Following the example of those such as Arnold Birch, the Chesterfield goalie who scored five penalties in the 1923–4 season, Higuita has scored over forty penalties in his career, and scored from a free kick when his team Atletico Nacional beat Pereira in the 1995 season. Goalkeepers scoring goals from goal kicks or long clearances is not unheard of, but to score goals in open play, as Peter Schmeichel of Manchester United did with his head from a corner in the UEFA Cup second round in 1995, is unusual.

Richmond Roose, goalkeeper for Stoke City, Everton and Sunderland, had a peculiar superstition. He thought that his luck would hold if he wore the same pair of shorts for the entire season, without having them washed. As he never won a championship medal or reached a Cup final during his playing career, despite being good enough to be selected twenty-four times for Wales, we can assume that his bizarre sartorial habits were not particularly lucky for him or his team-mates. One wonders whether the full story of his one season at Everton between spells at Stoke City was in some way connected with his smelly shorts. Stoke City actually finished one place higher than Everton in their Roose-less season, but were relegated to the Second Division as soon as he came back to the Potteries.

One of the most popular goalkeepers of all time was Bert Trautmann, Manchester City's German goalie, who had been a prisoner of war and then decided to make his career in England after the war. He had an enviable disciplinary record throughout his fourteen-year, 500-game career. In 1963, he was playing at Maine Road against West Ham, who were well on top against a City team that would end the season relegated to the Second Division. However, Trautmann and the City defence were convinced that West Ham's third goal was offside, and the goalkeeper protested so much that he was booked. The referee strode back to the centre circle and Trautmann turned to retrieve the ball from the back of the net. He picked it up, and drop-kicked it upfield with feeling. With unerring accuracy, the ball prescribed a savage arc and struck the ref in the middle of his back, and he fell winded to

35

the ground. The City faithful cheered, the referee tried to regain his dignity and Trautmann, realizing what was about to befall him, marched up to the spluttering official and handed him his jersey. He then turned and headed for the dressing room without waiting for his official dismissal.

Ryan Higgs, despite having a name that very nearly matched that of a footballer with some talent, let in twenty-nine goals in one match for Bracken Bank, a team in the Yorkshire Under-15 League, in the 1995–6 season. Despite this and the fact that it was Bracken Bank's thirteenth defeat in a row, he was still named Man of the Match. Tony Coton, who went on to play for Watford and Manchester City with distinction, did not win any awards on his debut in senior football, but he could hardly have faced a more daunting start. With his first touch of the ball after eighty-five seconds of the match between Birmingham City and Sunderland on 27 December 1980, the nineteen-year-old Coton, in the Birmingham goal, saved a penalty. Life was better for him than for Billy Callender, Crystal Palace's goalkeeper, who committed suicide at Palace's ground just before the start of the 1932–3 season.

Families are a feature of footballing history, to such an extent that even those players, like Julian Dicks, whom crowds would have us believe had no father, turn out to be the sons of footballing dads, in Julian's case, Alan Dicks. The most successful brothers in British football are probably the Charlton brothers, Bobby and Jack, who not only played together in the England side on many occasions in the 1960s, including the World Cup Final, but also each hold the record for most League appearances for their clubs. In Bobby's case, it was 606 appearances for Manchester United, and for Jack it was 629 appearances for Leeds United. Ivor and Len

Allchurch both played over 350 League games for Swansea in the 1950s and 1960s, and in all, they played more League games than the Charlton brothers – 1,293 against 1,235. They also played together for Wales eight times. Hong and Tao Xu were the first brothers to play for the Chinese national team, a particularly daring feat on the part of their parents, in a nation where having a second child is sternly frowned upon.

Football being a game for the young, it is a very rare thing for a father and son to play together at the highest levels. Alec Herd and David, his son, both in their time Scottish internationals, played together as inside forwards for Stockport County on 5 May 1951, in a 2–0 victory over Hartlepools United in a late-season Division Three (North) fixture. Alec was then thirty-nine years old, and David was just seventeen. Neither Herd scored. Almost forty years later, Hereford United's player-manager, Ian Bowyer, then thirty-eight, came on as substitute to join his eighteen-year-old son Gary playing an away fixture against Scunthorpe on 21 April 1990. The match ended in a 3–3 draw, with Gary Bowyer scoring one of Hereford's goals. Ten days later, they repeated the trick in a game at Aldershot, where Hereford won 2–0, although neither Bowyer got his name on the score sheet this time. Just seven weeks later, on 17 June, Bowyer senior resigned as manager at Hereford over a disagreement with the board about re-signing Gary to the club.

There has been one other father and son combination in League football in recent seasons. When Ayr United played Stranraer in a Scottish Second Division game in 1995, Tommy Sloan played as usual as Stranraer's striker. Ayr's mascot for the match was Sloan's eight-year-old son, Tommy junior.

Brothers playing against each other is a rare phenomenon, it only ever having happened once in an FA Cup Final (the

Rawsons in 1874), and not surprisingly it has never happened in an international, as far as records show. The Charlton brothers opposed each other in League matches often enough, of course, and twins Dean and David Holdsworth played against each other in the FA Cup in 1996, when Dean was with Wimbledon, which beat Watford, containing David. On Everton striker Bob Latchford's twenty-fourth birthday, he was leading Everton's forward line against Birmingham City. He scored two goals in a 3–0 victory, but it would be entirely unfair to suggest that they were a birthday gift from his brother Dave, Birmingham City's goalkeeper. On 17 February 1973, Wolverhampton Wanderers played Newcastle United in a First Division match, which ended at 1–1. The Wolves goal was scored by Kenny Hibbitt in the first half, but Newcastle pulled level after the interval with a fine strike by Terry Hibbitt, his brother. Ray Wilkins, player-manager of Queen's Park Rangers, and his brother Dean played against each other in a reserve team match and became the first brothers to be booked in the same incident. Big brother Ray fouled the younger Wilkins and was booked for the offence. While the referee's pencil was still in action, Dean took the resulting free kick, and was promptly booked for taking it too quickly. When Derek Clarke, playing for Leyton Orient against Carlisle United on 4 December 1976, conceded a penalty, his brother, Carlisle striker Frank Clarke, stepped up to take the spot kick. He missed. All the same, Carlisle won in the end, 1–0.

Footballers are lovable. Alan Ball has been quoted as saying that 'Some fellows who had the choice of a ball at their feet or a girl in their arms usually chose the girl. Not me. I never squeezed the spots on my face because I wanted to be repulsive and keep the girls away', but he is the exception to the rule. George Best was famous for his conquests, and at least two transfers involving major international stars came about because they were playing away rather too often for their manager's (and their girlfriend's) liking. Indeed, love is often a complication in football, rather than a help. Martin Allen was fined two weeks' wages by his manager at Queen's Park Rangers, Trevor Francis, for attending the birth of his son in March 1989, rather than playing football, and revelations about another QPR player, Andy Impey, imply that there is more to a footballer's life than merely scoring goals. Some clubs deliberately try to cultivate romance. When Fulham played Northampton Town on St Valentine's Day 1995, they were inundated with bookings for their package deal of a candlelit supper, roses, chocolates and tickets for the game. It ended in a 4–4 draw, watched by 3,423 people, the odd number meaning that either at least one fan was left on his or her own, or else there were some kinky goings-on. Lars Bohinen would know all about that sort of thing. When playing for Nottingham Forest, he was asked by a female fan to send a pair of his underpants, signed, to her. He claims he did

not comply with the request. But romance cannot conquer everything in football. For *Blind Date* contestant and Spurs fan Jeremy Steed, it was at the root of the problem. When asked for his opinion of his blind date, Georgia Rough *(sic)*, he said, 'She's a Millwall fan – need I say more? She showed a total lack of etiquette and courtesy.'

Many footballers are highly versatile. Trevor Bailey is one of very few men to play at Old Trafford in a top-class football match and in a cricket Test match. He played for Walthamstow Avenue when they played Manchester United in the fourth round of the FA Cup on 31 January 1953, and less than six months later played at Old Trafford in a Test Match against the Australians. Both games were drawn. Chris Balderstone played for Doncaster Rovers *v.* Brentford in a midweek evening game on 15 September 1975 while 51 not out overnight in a county game for Leicestershire. And Russell Osman, later an England football international, played rugby union in the afternoon of 19 March 1975 for England schoolboys against Wales at Twickenham, and then crossed London to play a game of soccer for the Ipswich youth team against

Arsenal in the evening. Dr Kevin O'Flanagan did even better than that, becoming in 1946 the first man to represent his country at both codes in one year. He played first for Ireland against France in the rugby union international in Dublin, then for Ireland against England under Association rules later in the year, his eighth of ten soccer caps for Ireland.

The best footballers are obviously very much in demand, and therefore often play for many teams during the course of their careers. Ernie Shepherd, while not perhaps among the greatest of footballers, nevertheless established a record in the 1948–9 season that is unlikely to be equalled. He began the season with Fulham, for which he played two games, one of which was drawn and the other lost. In December he moved to West Bromwich Albion, in a swap transfer involving Arthur Rowley, the highest scorer in the history of League football. Fulham's season went from strength to strength, but so did West Brom's. By the end of the season, Fulham and West Brom were the two clubs promoted from the Second Division to the top flight, but by then Shepherd had moved on to Hull City after just four games for the Throstles. Joining Hull in March 1949, he scored with his first kick for them, in the first minute of their match against Darlington, and stayed with them for the rest of the season as they too won promotion, from the Third Division to the Second. Ernie Shepherd is thus the only man to have played for three promoted clubs in one season.

Jim Oakes holds the unique record of playing for both teams in one League game. On 26 December 1932, he was picked as left back for Port Vale against Charlton Athletic. In those unfloodlit days, many games had to be abandoned if the light grew too bad, and only five days after the shortest day it came as no real surprise when the referee called it a day (or a night) before the ninety minutes were up. In January

1933, Oakes was sold to Charlton Athletic and when the original game was replayed at the end of the season in the better daylight of 26 April, he was playing for Charlton, who won 2–1. Not that it did them much good: relegation was already assured before that last but one game of the season, so no doubt Oakes wished he had stayed at Port Vale.

Tommy Lawton and Len Shackleton, two internationals who were very much in demand during the war years, led busy lives guesting for any team that was willing to pay for them. On Christmas Day 1940, Tommy Lawton played for Everton against Liverpool in the morning (ending up on the losing side by three goals to one), and in the afternoon played for Tranmere against Crewe, scoring both goals in a 2–2 draw. On the same day, Len Shackleton played for Bradford (Park Avenue) at Leeds in the morning (lost 2–1) and for Bradford City at Huddersfield in the afternoon, where he scored one goal in a 4–3 victory. On the same day, Brighton travelled to Norwich for a regional League game, but thanks to the rather difficult travel arrangements at Christmas in wartime, only five of the Brighton players turned up, and none of them was Lawton or Shackleton. Brighton hurriedly made up their side from Norwich City reserves and from servicemen in the crowd. Norwich were 10–0 up by half-time and finished winners by eighteen goals to nil, the biggest ever victory in an official game between two English League sides.

A year later, with wartime and Christmas still wreaking havoc on the fabric of southern England's public transport system (a pity that our railways can no longer use those excuses on a typical working weekday fifty years on), Bristol City travelled to the Dell to play against Southampton. Knowing that the trains might be troublesome, they set out in three cars, but only one of the three, containing two players and all the kit,

42

arrived. As there was a full house and eleven men to oppose them, the two Bristol City men had to find nine team-mates very quickly. Southampton sportingly loaned them five players, as well as their trainer, Gallagher, who had not played competitive football for several years. That made eight, and they found three others in the crowd – a soldier, a schoolmaster and an innocent bystander. The match kicked off a little late, and twenty minutes after it had begun the other two cars turned up. One car had suffered a puncture, the other had stopped to help, and then they had all got lost. No substitutions were allowed, so the nine City men just watched as Southampton beat them 5–2, the only consolation being in seeing Gallagher score his first goal in ages, against his own club.

Louis Monti has done better than any of these team-swapping turncoats. He played centre half for Argentina against Uruguay in the first World Cup Final, in Montevideo in 1930, and then for Italy against Czechoslovakia in the 1934 Final, in Rome. He gained only a runners-up medal with Argentina, but was a winner with Italy. When they retained the title in France four years later, Monti was no longer in the national side. Three players have won international caps for three countries, but none of them won World Cup medals. They are Ladislav Kubala, born in Hungary but subsequently also an international for Czechoslovakia and Spain; Jock Kennaway, who played for Scotland, Canada and the USA between 1928 and 1934; and the great Alfredo di Stefano, Argentine-born but also at different times a member of the Colombian and Spanish national teams.

Several players have played for at least two nations. Ferenc Puskas was one of several Hungarians who left their homeland in 1956 and went on to play for other countries, in his case Spain. R.E. Evans played ten games for Wales between 1906 and 1910 before it was discovered that he had been born in Chester and was therefore English. He played four times for England in 1911 and 1912. John Reynolds played for Ireland five times in 1890 and 1891 before switching to the mainland and playing eight games for England between 1892 and 1897. Tommy Davis played twice for the Republic of Ireland in 1936, once for Northern Ireland in 1937, and twice more for the Republic in 1938. Many other players have confusing qualifications. Matt Le Tissier is reputedly qualified to play for England, Scotland, Wales, Ireland and France, and Jeremy Goss, born in Cyprus and whose English family lives in Folkestone in Kent, was selected for Wales in April 1991.

Getting selected for your country, or any other country that will have you, is hard enough. Playing well at international level is even harder. Getting dropped after playing well is perhaps the most difficult feat of all, but it has been done. J.G. Veitch of the Wanderers was selected to play for England against Wales at Wrexham on 12 March 1894, a game in which the entire England side was made up of past, present or future members of the Wanderers. Veitch did all that could

have been asked of him, scoring a hat-trick in England's 5–1 victory. He never played for England again. Aston Villa's Eddie Lowe played three games as a half back for England in May 1947, against France, Switzerland and Portugal. The third game, against Portugal, ended 10–0 to England, but Lowe was dropped and never got back into the England side.

### EXTRA TIME

*Brothers in World Cup-winning teams*
Fritz and Otmar Walter, West Germany, 1934
Jack and Bobby Charlton, England, 1966

*Brothers in Olympic Gold Medal-winning teams*
Knut, Bertil and Gunnar Nordahl, Sweden, 1948

*Brothers in FA Cup-winning teams*
Frederick and Hubert Heron, Wanderers, 1876
Denis and Leslie Compton, Arsenal, 1950
Edward and George Robledo, Newcastle United, 1952
Brian and Jimmy Greenhoff, Manchester United, 1977

*Brothers playing against each other in a Cup Final*
William Rawson, Oxford University, and Lt Herbert Rawson, Royal Engineers, 1874. Oxford won 2–0.

*Three brothers in a League side*
Albert, Edward and Ralph Calland, Torquay United, 1952–3

William, John and George Carr, Middlesbrough, 1919–20
Jack, Alan and Herbert Keen for Barrow *v.* Port Vale, 31 August
1953
Joe, Tom and Harold Keetley, Doncaster Rovers, 1925–6
Rod, Ray and Danny Wallace, for Southampton, 17 games in
1988–9

*Two pairs of brothers on same team in FA Cup tie*
T. and R. Buzaglo, and L. and S. Wye, Woking *v.* Cambridge
United, 19 November 1988. Woking lost 4–1.

*Fathers and sons both gaining FA Cup winners' medals*
Peter Boyle, Sheffield United, 1899 and 1902, and Thomas Boyle,
Sheffield United, 1925
Harold Johnson, Sheffield United, 1899 and 1902, and Harold
Johnson Jr, Sheffield United, 1925
The Boyle and Johnson fathers played together on two Cup-
winning teams, and their sons played together to win the Cup
twenty-three years later. The fathers were internationals (Boyle for
Ireland, Johnson for England), the sons were not.
Jimmy Dunn, Everton, 1933, and Jimmy Dunn Jr,
Wolverhampton Wanderers, 1949
Alec Herd, Manchester City, 1934, and David Herd, Manchester
United, 1963

*Cousins playing in the same FA Cup Final*
Harold Pearson, West Bromwich Albion, and Harry Hibbs,
Birmingham City, both goalkeepers, 1931. WBA won 2–1.
Pearson's father (and Hibbs' uncle) had won a runners-up medal
as West Brom's goalkeeper in 1912.
Jim Baxter and Willie Cunningham, Preston North End, 1954.
PNE lost 3–2 to West Bromwich Albion.
Glyn Pardoe and Alan Oakes, Manchester City, 1969. City beat
Leicester City 1–0.
Clive and Paul Allen, Tottenham Hotspur, 1987. Spurs lost to
Coventry City 3–2.

*Cousins playing in consecutive FA Cup Finals*
Duncan Edwards, Manchester United, played in the 1957 Final
against Aston Villa. His cousin Dennis Stevens played in the 1958
Final for Bolton Wanderers against Manchester United, three
months after Edwards had died as a result of the Munich air crash.

*Twins in football*

John and George Fisher, born 19 June 1925. Both began their careers at Millwall.

Ron and Paul Futcher, born 25 September 1956. Both began their careers at Chester, and moved to Luton and then Manchester City together. Their elder brother Graham also played for Chester.

David and Dean Holdsworth, born 8 November 1968. Both began at Watford.

David and Peter Jackson, born 23 February 1937. Both played for Wrexham, Bradford City and Tranmere Rovers.

Alan and Garry Kimble, born 6 August 1966. Both played for Charlton Athletic, Exeter City and Cambridge United.

47

John and Brian Linighan, born 2 November 1973. Both began at Sheffield Wednesday.

David (Carlisle United, 1995–6) and Alan Reeves (Wimbledon 1995–6), born 19 November 1967.

Alf and John Stevens, born 13 June 1919. Both played for Leeds United and Swindon Town.

Ray and Rodney Wallace, born 2 October 1969. Both began at Southampton and moved to Leeds Utd. Their elder brother Danny played with them at Southampton.

*Large families in football*

*Barkas*: brothers Ned, Frank, Sam and Tom all played League football before and after the war.

*Clarke*: brothers Frank, Alan, Derek, Kelvin and Wayne all played League football between 1961, when Frank was nineteen, and 1996, when Wayne was thirty-five. All five experienced relegation at least once.

*Keetley*: brothers Frank, Harold, Joe, Tom and Albert all played League football, many of them for Doncaster Rovers.

*Linighan*: father Brian, sons Andy, David, John and Brian all played League football, beginning at Hartlepool, where they were all born.

*McLaren*: four McLaren brothers were on League teams' books in the 1950s, all as goalkeepers, but only three – David, Roy and Scott – actually played League football.

*Milburn*: brothers George, Jimmy, John and Stan, as well as their first cousin Jackie, all played League football before and after the war. The brothers' nephews, Jack and Bobby Charlton, also played League football.

*Moore*: brothers Norman and Tom played for Grimsby Town after the war. Norman's sons Andy, David and Kevin all played for Grimsby Town between 1976 and 1986.

*Wallbanks*: brothers Jack, Fred, Jim, Horace and Harry all played League football between 1929 and 1952.

*Wilkins*: father George played League football before and after the war. Sons Graham, Ray and Dean all played since 1972.

*Goalkeeper who failed to turn up because nobody told him he was playing*
Perry Digweed, Brighton and Hove Albion *v.* Bournemouth, 10 September 1988

*Goalkeepers who have scored goals in open play*
Ray Charles, East Fife, 1990
D.J. Day, Bourne Grammar School, 1949
Andy Goram, Hibernian, 1988
Iain Hesford, Maidstone, 1991
Pat Jennings, Tottenham Hotspur, 1967
Steve Ogrizovic, Coventry City, 1986
Michelangelo Rampulla, Cremonese, 1992
Peter Schmeichel, Manchester United, 1995
Steve Sherwood, Watford, 1984
Peter Shilton, Leicester City, 1967
Albert Uytenbogaardt, Charlton Athletic Reserves, 1950
Charles Williams, Manchester City, 1897

*Reasons for being elected Footballer of the Year*
'How could I avoid being Footballer of the Year playing behind our defence?' – Pat Jennings, Tottenham Hotspur goalkeeper, 1973

# INTRODUCTION TO MANAGEMENT

## 3

When the top stars in most sports retire, they take up something innocent, like writing about the game they served so well, or administering it for the next generation, or perhaps they turn to the obscurity of running a pub or a wastepaper recycling business. Footballers are different. As soon as they retire from the playing field, and in some cases even before they hang up their boots for the last time, they go into football management. There seems to be no exception to the rule – all footballers go into football management. Some of them start as third team coaches, or scouts or 'back room boys' (which means it's cheaper to keep them on the books than go through an industrial tribunal for wrongful dismissal), but a select few start at the top. Alec Stock, a very successful manager in the 1960s and 1970s, began at Yeovil Town, and many years later was quoted as saying, 'I thought you had to have experience. You don't. The great thing is to cut yourself in at the top. Experience crucifies people.'

Football management crucifies people. Stock himself was fired by Queen's Park Rangers from his hospital bed in 1968, since when QPR have averaged a new manager every other season, despite spending most of that time in the top division, a fine achievement for a comparatively small club. Not many managers have spent as short a time at the helm as the three days that Bill Lambton did with Second Division Scunthorpe

United in 1959 (he lasted a little longer at Leeds United and Chester), but his period in charge is nearer the average tenure than Fred Everiss' record forty-six years (1902–48) in charge of West Bromwich Albion, during which time his club was promoted twice and relegated three times, but won the League title for the only time in its history, in 1919–20, and the FA Cup once, in 1931. Everiss had been with the club since 1896, first as a player, then as secretary before becoming manager, and after he stepped down, the following forty-six years saw West Brom go through twenty-one managerial changes. Other clubs have left the same man in charge for many years, notably George Ramsay for forty-two years at Aston Villa (1884–1926), Matt Busby's twenty-four years at Manchester United, and Jimmy Seed's twenty-three years at Charlton Athletic, from 1933 to 1956. Seed presided over the most successful period in Charlton's history, which goes some way to explaining his longevity, but for him 1947 was the make-or-break year. Actually, it was the make and break year, because just after Charlton Athletic had put themselves in the FA Cup record books by becoming the tenth club to win the Cup after losing in the final the previous year, Jimmy Seed dropped the cup and broke the lid.

Seed's playing career was spent mainly at Tottenham, where he was club captain and played five times for England in the early 1920s. He also won a Cup winners' medal in 1921, putting him on the comparatively short list of men who have both played for and managed Cup-winning sides. He enjoyed the even more exclusive distinction, as captain of Spurs, of once ordering the referee off the pitch in a League game. It was a hot day in an early season fixture, so the referee was not wearing a jacket, as was then the custom. His white shirt clashed with the Spurs colours, and after too many players

had passed the ball to the ref, Seed asked him to go and find a dark top before the game could continue. If his career as a player was no more than averagely good, Seed's record as a football club manager must rank among the greatest. He took over at Charlton when they were in the Third Division (South), having just been relegated after finishing bottom of the Second Division in 1932–3. They were then definitely one of London's least glamorous clubs, but Seed restructured them so quickly and so well that within two years they won the Third Division (South) title by eight points. The next season, they came second in the Second Division, just one point behind the champions Manchester United, and then in 1936–7, in their first season ever in the top division, they finished second to Manchester City by a mere three points. Until the war, they remained one of Britain's top four clubs, and in their final League game before the war finished organized football for eight seasons, they beat Manchester United 2–0. Jimmy Seed carried on as manager after the war, immediately leading the Haddicks to two successive FA Cup Finals, in 1946 and 1947.

He remained as their manager until he retired in 1956. Throughout his time at the Valley, he had never had to worry about who to select as goalkeeper. From 1934 to 1956, Sam Bartram played in Charlton's goal in 583 League games out of the 630 they played in those fifteen seasons. In 1957, under new management, Charlton Athletic came bottom of the First Division by seven clear points and returned to the Second Division.

52   Several other Football League managers would claim to have been at least as successful as Jimmy Seed. Irishman Billy McCandless held the unlikely distinction of managing three separate Welsh teams in the English Third Division (South) championship. He led Newport County to the title in 1938–9, the only title Newport ever won, then managed Cardiff City when they won the title in 1946–7. He completed his hat-trick with Swansea in 1948–9. He never got round to managing Wrexham.

Bob Paisley managed Liverpool from 1974 to 1983, during which period the club won the League title six times, the FA Cup once, the League Cup three times, the European Cup three times, the UEFA Cup once, the Super Cup once and were runners-up in the World Club Championship once. More importantly, during Paisley's period as manager of Liverpool, Everton won nothing. Sir Alf Ramsey is still the only man to have managed the same club, Ipswich Town, to the championship of three divisions. He guided Ipswich to the Third Division (South) title on goal average in 1956–7, they won the Second Division by a clear point in 1960–1, and the very next season they won the League Championship, three points ahead of the runners-up, Burnley. Four years later, Ramsey also won the World Cup as England's manager, thus earning himself a knighthood.

One of his successors in the England hot seat, Graham Taylor, also had a remarkably successful club managerial career. His time at Watford from 1977 to 1987 began with the Championship of the Fourth Division in his first season in charge. The next season, they were runners-up in the Third Division, earning a second successive promotion, and they also reached the semi-final of the League Cup. It then took them three seasons to climb out of the Second Division, finishing second behind Luton Town in 1981–2. In their first season in the top division, Taylor just failed to emulate Sir Alf's achievement. Watford came second, the position that Ipswich Town had occupied the previous two seasons, behind Liverpool but one point ahead of Manchester United. In 1984 they reached the FA Cup Final, but the season after Taylor left to manage Aston Villa they slipped back down to the Second Division. With Aston Villa, Taylor was once again runner-up for the League title, once again behind Liverpool. Taylor has thus managed two clubs that have just missed the League title, which puts him behind three other names on management's all-time roll of honour.

Herbert Chapman, Brian Clough and Kenny Dalglish have all won the League title with two different clubs. No manager has yet guided a team to a hat-trick of League titles, but Herbert Chapman remains the only person ever to have managed two teams that won the League title two years in a row – a feat he achieved with Huddersfield Town in 1923–4 and 1924–5 and then with Arsenal in 1932–3 and 1933–4. Both teams went on to complete a hat-trick of titles, but under different managers. When Chapman left Huddersfield Town, Cecil Potter took the team on to their hat-trick in his only season in charge, and when Chapman died in 1934, George Allison took over the successful Arsenal side that Chapman

53

had left behind. The only other team to have completed a hat-trick of League titles, Liverpool, also did so under two managers, Bob Paisley in 1981–2 and 1982–3, and Joe Fagan in 1983–4. The man who established Liverpool as a great force in post-war football, Bill Shankly, never managed his team to three consecutive championships, despite the fact that he, like Chapman, had managed Huddersfield for several seasons. Shankly's career as a manager had begun after a playing career with Preston North End and five caps for Scotland, at Carlisle, and then he spent time in charge of Grimsby and Workington (where there was no electric light), before Huddersfield and then Liverpool. Lawrie McMenemy, who spent twelve very successful seasons in charge of Southampton from 1973 to 1985, began as assistant manager at Gateshead, which had just been kicked out of the League. It is not all glamour in the managerial hot seat.

Kenny Dalglish started at absolutely the other end of the scale. He is the only person to have guided a team to the double as player-manager, which he did with Liverpool in 1985–6, his very first season in charge. He was also, as a player, a member of two Celtic double-winning teams in the 1970s. Alex Ferguson, who managed Manchester United to the double in 1993–4 and 1995–6, also managed Aberdeen to the Scottish double in 1983–4, making him the only person ever to have managed two double-winning teams, one on each side of the border. He is also the only British manager to have won the European Cup Winners' Cup with two teams. Jimmy Cochrane, who managed Kilmarnock in 1929 and Sunderland in 1937, is the only other man to have managed Cup winners on both sides of the border. Even these achievements are nothing next to the record of Ernst Happel, an Austrian who led three different teams from three different countries to their national League titles and then to European Cup Finals. In 1970, he managed the Dutch club Feyenoord, which beat Celtic in the European Cup Final. Eight years later, he was with the Belgian champions FC Brugge, which lost in the final, at Wembley, to a Kenny Dalglish goal for Liverpool. In that year he also took the Dutch national side to the World Cup Final, where they lost in extra time to Argentina. In 1983, he was at the helm of Hamburg, which beat Juventus in Athens to win one more European title. In a career that spanned six countries over thirty-four years, Happel won seventeen international and domestic titles.

Brian Clough managed over one thousand League games in a career that covered Hartlepool, Derby County, Leeds, Brighton and Nottingham Forest. His one-thousandth game as manager was with Notts Forest against Spurs at White Hart Lane on 30 December 1989, which Forest won 3–2. During his time as a manager he won the Second Division title with Derby County, as well as four League Cups, two European

Cups and the European Super Cup with Notts Forest, as well as his two League titles. Jim Smith is another of the select few who have been in charge for more than one thousand League games in all, with Birmingham City, Blackburn Rovers, Colchester, Derby County, Newcastle, Oxford, Portsmouth and Queen's Park Rangers. In twenty-five years of trying, he won promotion five times with four clubs but never won a major title.

56

Smith, known as The Bald Eagle, has sacrificed his hair to his profession, as has Bob Stokoe, who most famously managed Sunderland, then a Second Division club, to a Cup Final victory over the all-conquering Leeds United in 1973. In a career as long as Smith's, Stokoe has not only reached the heights with Sunderland, but has also seen the lower reaches of the League tables in three separate stints at Carlisle United, two at Blackpool, two at Rochdale and two at Bury. Managers often seem to return to the scene of their past crimes, as though being sacked once is not enough. When Stokoe was manager at Rochdale for the second time in 1979–80, he fined his players half a week's wages after they lost 5–1 at Tranmere on 25 January 1980. The Professional Footballers' Association claimed that this action was illegal. 'You cannot fine players for bad performances,' was the union view, and perhaps they were right. Stokoe lasted only a few more months at Rochdale, which remained steadfastly in the Fourth Division for twelve more seasons.

If the players are consistently turning in bad performances, it is possible that the manager is not doing his job properly. The Firth Moor Flyers Under-18s, playing in the BCR Boxes Auckland and District League, are among the worst clubs in Britain, having in one season conceded 113 goals in their first eight games, while scoring only five goals. Played eight lost

eight usually results in no points, but in Firth Moor's case, thanks to managerial and administrative problems, they had nine points deducted, leaving them on minus nine and deep in the relegation zone.

Like any other job, football management is a matter of attention to detail, going to endless trouble to get things right. The example of Gary Johnson, then assistant manager at Cambridge United, is a typical one. At the beginning of 1991, his team was drawn against Wolverhampton Wanderers in the FA Cup third round. As Wolves were a division higher than Cambridge at the time, there was no first-hand up-to-date information available on them. But the enterprising Johnson was not to be defeated by such trifles. He telephoned the Wolves Clubcall telephone line to find out all Cambridge needed to know, and they travelled to Molineux secure in the knowledge that they had left no stone unturned in their preparation for the big game. Cambridge won 1–0, and Johnson remarked that 'It was forty-nine pence very well spent.'

Management can cause people to do and say daft things. Alec Stock said in 1975 that terrace violence was sickening.

'The only answer is for decent supporters to become vigilantes on the terraces. A few thumps on the nose would soon put a stop to these silly youngsters.' His advice has been taken by several of his colleagues. Brian Clough struck a fan after Notts Forest's 5–2 victory over Queen's Park Rangers in the Littlewoods Cup on 18 January 1989. And after a particularly disappointing 3–2 defeat at Luton, Grimsby manager Brian Laws threw a plate at his Italian striker Ivano Bonetti in the dressing room on 10 February 1996 and broke the poor man's jaw. York manager John Bird and Scarborough manager Ray McHale were banned from the touchline for three months for aiming punches at each other after Scarborough had lost 3–1 at home to their Yorkshire neighbours on 24 November 1989. Rather surprisingly, they were still managing their respective clubs when the ban ended. McHale, indeed, lasted until 1993 and then returned to Scarborough little over a year, and three managers, later.

Management is a very precarious business. Kevin Cullis lasted as manager of Swansea City for only seven days in February 1996, having taken over because the previous man-

ager, Bobby Smith, had been ordered to pay out of his own money for a set of rubber-soled boots for his players to wear on hard pitches, and so resigned in disgust. Cullis had no experience of top-class football, either as a player or manager, but he was in charge of Cradley Town's youth team for four years, which seems as good a background as any for taking over at Swansea. Maybe they mistook him for Stan Cullis, manager of Wolverhampton Wanderers during their glory years between 1948 and 1964, and of Birmingham City for five years after that. Kevin Cullis was quoted as describing his new job as 'the biggest challenge in football. I aim to take this club back to where it was ten or fifteen years ago.' This was probably the reason he was fired so quickly. Fifteen years earlier, Swansea had been in the top division, but ten years earlier, they had been on their way out of the Third Division and into the Fourth. A manager who cannot decide whether to aim for the top or the bottom is unlikely to last for long.

Tim Ward's stay at Exeter in 1953 is variously listed as something between a week and twenty-five days, yet he was an England international and not a bad manager. After leaving Exeter, he moved to Barnsley, where he spent seven years as manager, to Carlisle United and Derby County. Jimmy McIlroy lasted just eighteen days at Bolton in 1970, and Johnny Cochrane spent a mere thirteen days at Reading in 1939, immediately after eleven very successful years in charge at Sunderland. It is, not surprisingly, the least successful clubs that get through managers at the fastest rate. While Liverpool had only thirteen managers in their first hundred years as a League club, and Manchester United have had only seven since the war, Darlington have had twenty-eight in the post-war period, at an average of just under two seasons each. Southampton never sacked a manager until Chris Nicholl got the bullet in 1991: he was their seventeenth manager. Their eighteenth, Ian Branfoot, and their nineteenth, Dave Merrington, were also fired. One of Nicholl's and Branfoot's predecessors at Southampton, Lawrie McMenemy, said that the difference between management at the top and at the bottom is that 'I don't eat so much fish. I eat more fillet steak. It's as simple as that.' Branfoot moved promptly from Southampton to the manager's chair at Fulham, so he had to get used to fish again. He didn't have to worry about whether the Fulham fans would take to him, though. Within weeks the Southampton fans had offered to sell their excess stocks of 'Branfoot Out' T-shirts to the Craven Cottage faithful.

If a manager cannot build a successful team, he will not last long. The most important ingredient in becoming a successful manager is skill at playing the transfer market. When Burnley played Gainsborough Trinity in the second round of the FA Cup on 1 February 1913, they won 4–1, but their manager John Haworth decided that the Gainsborough defensive skills were just what Burnley needed. He therefore bought the Gainsborough goalie and both their full backs. Despite the fact, or perhaps because of the fact, that these players were cup-tied for that year, Burnley progressed to the semi-finals before losing to Sunderland after a replay. The next season, with the Gainsborough defence now firmly ensconced in their starting line-up, Haworth led Burnley to the Cup Final at Crystal Palace, where they beat Liverpool 1–0 to take the Cup for the only time in their history. Just after the First World War, Haworth proved he had lost none of his flair by signing Jack Bruton, a miner, at the pithead of the mine in which he worked. When Bruton moved to Blackburn Rovers in 1929, he earned Burnley £6,500, the biggest fee ever paid by Blackburn at that time.

Dick Ray, who managed Leeds United from 1927 to 1935, tried to sign Wilcockson of York City in 1934, and travelled to York to put the finishing touches to the deal. York City were happy to sell the player, but Wilcockson himself was not there. He was in London, where his family lived. Ray travelled to the Wilcockson family home, to be told that the player had gone to the cinema, but they were not sure which one. Ray then went to all the cinemas in the district and got the managers to flash an urgent message on their screens. Finally, he tracked down his man, and the transfer forms were signed in the cinema manager's office.

Whether you are starting with £10 million or £10, if you can put together a team that will increase in value under your management, you will be a successful manager. Darlington manager Jack English spent only £80 putting together the team that won the Third Division (North) title in 1924–5, the only title that Darlington ever won. All of that vast sum was spent on one player, their top scorer David Brown, who that season established a League record by scoring thirty-nine goals, which was exactly half of his side's total of seventy-eight for the season. Manager English had spent just £1 0s 6d per goal that year, which is rather less than the hundreds of thousands of pounds per goal spent on leading strikers in the Premiership seventy years on. Even allowing for inflation, English was a canny manager.

So was Sunderland's Bob Kyle, who sold their star forward Charles Buchan to the newly appointed Herbert Chapman of Arsenal in 1925. The fee was £2,000, enormous in those days, but he added a rider that meant that Sunderland earned an extra £100 for every goal that Buchan scored for Arsenal that season. He scored nineteen, twenty-one or twenty-two, depending on which authority you go by, so the final fee was doubled, to around £4,000. What was more, the thirty-three-year-old Buchan was by now nearing the end of his career, having won a Championship medal and a Cup runners-up medal with Sunderland in 1912–13, and the last of his six England caps in 1924. He won another FA Cup runners-up medal with Arsenal in 1927, but by the time Arsenal began their great years of the 1930s, Buchan had retired.

This type of 'add-on' deal is becoming more common now, as the smaller clubs have to realize the full potential of their young players in the transfer market. All the same, Hayes could hardly believe their luck when Les Ferdinand, whom they had sold to Queen's Park Rangers in April 1987, moved to Newcastle United for £6 million in 1995. Hayes had an agreement that they would take 10 per cent of any onward transfer fee, so they suddenly found themselves with a windfall of over half a million pounds.

Brian Clough was the first manager to spend £1 million on a player when he bought Trevor Francis from Birmingham City on 9 February 1979. Officially, the fee was actually

£975,000, but with a 10 per cent levy and 8 per cent VAT added on, it worked out at £1,150,500. In 1995–6, the total amount of money spent on players into and out of English League clubs topped £250 million for the first time, a four-fold increase in just six years. Yet not too long ago there were still some astonishing bargains to be found. Nineteen-year-old Tony Cascarino was spotted by Gillingham manager Keith Peacock in 1982, playing for Crockenhill in the Kent League. Gillingham were not then one of the wealthiest clubs in the League, so Gillingham and Crockenhill agreed that a fair price for this precocious striker would be twelve new tracksuits, two footballs and some corrugated iron for the Crockenhill ground. Cascarino went on to Millwall and then to Aston Villa in 1990, this time for a fee of £1,500,000, which represented about one-fortieth of the entire expenditure on transfers that season, and could have bought twelve cloth-of-gold tracksuits, as well as several hundred footballs and still have left enough over to fence the entire ground.

63

This was not the first time that such a deal had been done. In 1927, Manchester United bought half back Hughie McLenahan from Stockport County in return for a gallon or two of ice-cream. In 1931, Mossend Celtic, a Lanarkshire junior club, sold Jock Spelton to Holytown United for fifty sheets of corrugated iron. And when Arsenal signed the teenaged Len Shackleton as an amateur in the 1930s, the cost was his football boots, which Arsenal had to buy from his former club, which owned them. Blackpool signed local teenager J. William Wright in May 1950, giving his club a set of Blackpool's famous tangerine shirts and shorts in exchange. Wright was a winger who only played fifteen games in five years with the club before moving on to no greater success at Leicester City, so it may be argued that his local club got the

better of the deal. Irishman Jimmy O'Neill's move from Everton to Stoke City towards the end of his career in 1960 was marked by a signing-on fee consisting of a new cooker.

## EXTRA TIME

*Foreign managers at English League clubs*
Ossie Ardiles (Argentina) managed Swindon Town, 1989–91, Newcastle United, 1991–92 and Tottenham Hotspur 1993–94.
Danny Bergara (Uruguay) managed Rochdale, 1988–9, and Stockport Co., 1989–95.
Ruud Gullit (Netherlands) managed Chelsea from 1996.
Dr Jozef Venglos, from Czechoslovakia, managed Aston Villa, 1990–1.

*Managers who have won the League title with different clubs*
Herbert Chapman, Huddersfield, 1923–4, 1924–5 and Arsenal 1930–1, 1932–3, 1933–4. Chapman died before Arsenal completed their hat-trick in 1934–5.
Brian Clough, Derby County, 1971–2 and Notts Forest 1977–8. He was also briefly manager of defending champions Leeds United in 1974.
Kenny Dalglish, Liverpool, 1985–6, 1987–8, 1989–90 and Blackburn Rovers, 1994–5. Liverpool did the double in his first season as manager.

*Managers who have managed more than five League clubs*
8 – Tommy Docherty (Aston Villa, Chelsea, Derby County, Manchester United, Preston North End, Queen's Park Rangers, Rotherham United, Wolverhampton Wanderers. Docherty also managed Scotland, two Australian clubs, Oporto of Portugal and non-League Altrincham)
8 – Jim Smith (Birmingham City, Blackburn Rovers, Colchester United, Derby County, Newcastle United, Oxford United, Portsmouth, Queen's Park Rangers)
7 – John Bond (Birmingham City, AFC Bournemouth, Burnley, Manchester City, Norwich City, Shrewsbury Town, Swansea City)
7 – Allan Brown (Blackpool, Bury, Luton Town, Nottingham Forest, Southport, Torquay United, Wigan Athletic)
7 – Major Frank Buckley (Blackpool, Hull City, Leeds United, Norwich City, Notts County, Walsall, Wolverhampton Wanderers)
6 – Len Ashurst (Cardiff City [twice], Gillingham, Hartlepool United, Newport County, Sheffield Wednesday, Sunderland)
6 – Ron Atkinson (Aston Villa, Cambridge United, Coventry City, Manchester United, Sheffield Wednesday, West Bromwich Albion [twice])
6 – Ron Saunders (Aston Villa, Birmingham City, Manchester City, Norwich City, Oxford United, West Bromwich Albion)
6 – Bob Stokoe (Blackpool [twice], Bury [twice], Charlton Athletic, Carlisle United [three times], Rochdale [twice], Sunderland)

*Brothers as managers of League clubs*
Brian Little, manager of Leicester City and Aston Villa, is the brother of York City manager Alan Little.

*Father and son managing same League club*
Bill Dodgin Sr managed Brentford, 1953–7. His son Bill Dodgin Jr managed Brentford 1976–80.

*Brothers opposing each other as managers in Scottish Cup Final*
Motherwell, managed by Tommy McLean, beat Dundee United, managed by Jim McLean, 4–3 in the 1991 Final.

*Manager sacked while 'Manager of the Month'*
Mike Walker, sacked by Fourth Division Colchester in October 1987

*Managerial excuses for defeat*

Airdrieonians 1, Aberdeen 2, 10 August 1991. Airdrie manager Alex MacDonald said, 'We ended up playing football, and that's not our style.'

Coventry City 0, Wimbledon 1, 31 August 1991. Coventry manager Terry Butcher said, 'I'd like to apologize to all the fans who paid good money to watch that. If that game is the future of British football, I want no part of it.'

Manchester City 10, Huddersfield Town 1, Second Division, 7 November 1987. Huddersfield manager Malcolm McDonald said, 'At least three of their goals were offside.'

Sweden 2, England 1, 17 June 1992. England manager Graham Taylor said, 'We could have done with not having half-time, but you have to have half-time.'

# THE ODD GOAL

## 4

Pelé scored over one thousand of them; Arthur Rowley scored 434 in a League career that stretched from 1946 to 1965; Jimmy McGrory scored 410 in only 408 Scottish League games; the second of three that Geoff Hurst scored for England in the 1966 World Cup Final at Wembley is still hotly disputed three decades on. Ian Rush scored his first and his two hundredth for Liverpool past the same goalkeeper – John Lukic, who was playing for Arsenal when Rush first struck in 1981, and for Leeds United when the double century came up on 28 August 1993. John Petrie of Arbroath scored thirteen of his team's thirty-six in one match against Bon Accord. The *Dundee Courier and Argus* reported that 'Milne, the active goalkeeper of the Arbroath, neither touched

the ball with hand or foot during the match, but remained under the friendly shelter of an umbrella the whole time.' On exactly the same day, 5 September 1885, Dundee Harp put thirty-five past Aberdeen Rovers' defence, these being two of the highest scores ever recorded in officially organized matches. Goals are the only thing that count in football.

Sometimes, though, even goals don't count. When Bournemouth scored ten against Northampton Town in the Third Division (South) to record their biggest ever League victory, they might perhaps have guessed that the achievement would not be listed in the record books. The match took place on Saturday, 2 September 1939, Bournemouth and Boscombe Athletic's third game of the 1939–40 season. By the time the Monday newspapers reported the results, they were devoting rather more space to the event that led to the cancellation of that year's Football League programme – the declaration of war against Germany, some eighteen hours after the tenth Bournemouth goal had hit the back of the Northampton net. So Jack Kirkham's hat-trick, Paddy Gallacher's double, Bob Redfern's two, as well as the goals from Fred Marsden, Bill Tunnicliffe and Tommy Payton were never officially noted in the League annals. Nor, for that matter, were Ted Drake's four in Arsenal's 5–2 thrashing of Sunderland the same day, or Bowden's three of Newcastle's eight against Swansea.

Denis Law knows the feeling only too well. On 28 January 1961, Manchester City played Luton Town at Kenilworth Road in the fourth round of the FA Cup. Manchester City were hoping for a straightforward game, having been taken to two replays in the previous round, before coming through 2–0 against Cardiff City. But the fates were against them. This time it was not an invasion of Poland that prevented his team's feat from entering the record books, but the weather. It was atrocious, with rain pouring down almost all day. There was some doubt about whether the match would go ahead, but in the end it began on time and on a pitch that soon became too muddy for a normal passing game. Luton were the first to adapt to the conditions, and within the first twenty minutes they were 2–0 up. Then Law came into his own. Over the next fifty minutes he scored six goals and, with twenty minutes to go, Manchester were 6–2 up and apparently coasting on a sea of mud into the fifth round. But by this time the conditions were so bad that play could not continue. After sixty-nine minutes the referee, Ken Tuck, abandoned the game and a replay was set for two days later. The pitch was still muddy, but this time Law could not work his magic, and Manchester City were beaten 3–1. Law scored the only City goal, but this was small compensation for having six Cup goals written out of history by the weather.

A day of rather better weather was 30 September 1989, when there were seven hat-tricks scored in English and Scottish League matches, all of which counted. Alex Rae of Falkirk scored four goals against Albion Rovers, while Steve Claridge (Aldershot *v.* Scunthorpe), Simon Garner (Blackburn *v.* Barnsley), Charlie Gibson (Dumbarton *v.* Cowdenbeath), Gary Lineker (Spurs *v.* QPR), Lee Turnbull (Doncaster *v.* Hartlepool) and Bobby Williamson (Rotherham *v.* Cardiff) all scored three. If you score three goals in a game, tradition says that you are allowed to keep the ball. When Trevor Senior scored three for Reading against Cardiff City in an early season Third Division game on 31 August 1985, he asked for the match ball after the game and was told by Cardiff officials that it would cost £40. Reading had the last laugh, though. At the end of the season they won the divisional title, while Cardiff were relegated to the Fourth Division.

Hat-tricks are no longer a particular curiosity – Alan Shearer, the first man in fifty years to score thirty goals in each of three consecutive top division seasons, hit three within the space of ten Premiership games in Blackburn's championship season, 1994–5 – but to hit three in four games is more remarkable. This feat was achieved by Manchester City's Holford in 1909. On 9 January that year, Manchester City beat Bradford City 4–3, Holford hitting three. On 16 January, they lost 4–3 to Tottenham Hotspur in the FA Cup, but Holford scored all three, oddly the only goals he ever scored for Manchester City in the Cup. A week later, City lost 3–1 away to Manchester United, but another week later, on 30 January, Holford hit three more, this time in a 4–0 victory against Everton.

Goals are sometimes much harder to come by. Queen's Park of Glasgow never conceded a goal in their first seven years of existence. They were formed in 1867, and did not concede their first goal until 16 January 1875. Although they entered the FA Cup in nine of its first thirteen years of existence, they did not concede a goal in that competition until 29 December

1883, when Foulkes of Oswestry Town scored as his side went down 7–1 to Queen's Park in the third round. Coventry City, in the Second Division in the 1919–20 season, went for eleven matches over eighty-one days without scoring a goal. On 4 October 1919, they lost 2–1 at home to Leicester City, but this was the last League goal they were to score until Christmas Day. In the meantime they lost 1–0 at home to Fulham and drew 0–0 at Craven Cottage, drew 0–0 at home to Brentford, lost 1–0 at Bristol City, lost 2–0 at home and then 5–0 away, both to Huddersfield. Blackpool held them to a 0–0 draw at Coventry before beating them 2–0 in the return a week later. Then they met West Ham, both at home and away, drawing 0–0 at home and losing 2–0 away. On 20 December, they drew 0–0 at home against Clapton Orient, by which time their long-suffering fans had seen one goal in six home games. On Christmas Day, they found their goal-scoring touch again, beating Stoke 3–2, but then Christmas has always been the time for goals in football.

71

Football matches were played regularly on Christmas Day between 1899 (when Preston North End beat Aston Villa 3–2 in the first ever Christmas Day League match) and 1959. The Christmas period is traditionally a time of gifts for forwards, and stuffing for goalkeepers. As early as 1909, Wycombe Wanderers, then in the Great Western Suburban League, beat Staines 18–1 on 27 December, and the next day beat the Second Scots Guards 8–1. The biggest ever League score is Tranmere Rovers' 13–4 win over Oldham (who scarcely lived up to their Athletic suffix), which happened on Boxing Day in 1935. Tranmere forward 'Bunny' Bell scored nine, but missed a second-half penalty kick. Exactly twenty-seven years later, Oldham got the Christmas message at last and put eleven past the Southport defence, with Bert Lister scoring six of them.

At Christmas, teams often play home and away fixtures within days of each other, and the result of the first game is no indicator of the result in the return fixture. Over Christmas 1960, Plymouth Argyle lost 6–4 at Charlton, but the next day beat them 6–4 at Home Park, with Wilf Carter scoring five of them. On Boxing Day 1963, Fulham beat Ipswich 10–1 (four goals from Graham Leggat, three from Bobby Howfield and one each from Maurice Cook, Alan Mullery and Bobby Robson). Three of Leggat's goals came within three minutes between the seventeenth and twentieth minutes of the first half, the fastest hat-trick ever scored in the top division. On the same day, Blackburn Rovers came to Upton Park and carved up the home side 8–2. Two days later, Ipswich won the return against Fulham at Portman Road 4–2, while West Ham went up to Ewood Park and beat Blackburn 3–1.

Defenders are obviously not at their best over the holiday period. Why they should suffer more than the forwards from an excess of good cheer is anybody's guess, but it remains an incontrovertible fact, backed up by an impressive array of weird statistics. Michael Parkinson remembers Dave Lindsay, Barnsley's centre half in the early 1950s, going to take a free kick in a League game on Boxing Day. He put the ball down in the right place, near the touchline. He then stepped back a few yards, measuring his run-up to the ball, and fell over the low wall that circled the playing area. For some time nothing could be seen of him except a pair of legs sticking over the top of the wall. The referee moved across to investigate, and found Lindsay lying on the ground, apparently asleep. 'Let him lie there,' shouted a voice from the terraces. 'He's happy. And so are we.'

Perhaps Lindsay was feeling the need to sleep off the turkey and Christmas pudding. If so, he might have done better to

follow the precedent of Ambrose Brown of Wrexham, who was sent off on Christmas Day in 1936 after just thirty seconds in the match at Hull City. That gave him eighty-nine minutes and thirty seconds more rest than the remainder of his side, but Hull, in his absence, failed to reap the usual Yuletide harvest of goals. They put just one goal past the Wrexham goalkeeper, the lowest tally of the day in the Third Division (North). Eleven players against ten at Christmas is obviously a close contest, but fourteen against eight is less equal. On 26 December 1952, West Bromwich Albion played Sheffield Wednesday and won 5–4. A good, close contest, you might well think. But of the nine goals, seven were scored by Sheffield Wednesday players. West Brom managed two of their own, but without own goals from both Wednesday full backs, Norman Curtis and Vince Kenny, and another from wing half Eddie Gannon, they would have lost the match 4–2. Kenny did not score a single goal at the right end in a career stretching over eight seasons with Sheffield Wednesday. Two years later, on Christmas Day 1954, Carlisle United beat Rochdale 7–2. Rochdale players scored five of the goals, thanks to own goals by Henry Boyle, Danny Murphy and George Underwood. None of the three players ever scored a goal for Rochdale, in a combined League career of 303 matches. Carlisle finished twentieth in the Third Division (North) that season, but without Rochdale's Christmas generosity they would have had to apply for re-election.

The Scottish club Motherwell first reached the Scottish Cup Final in 1931, when they were up against the mighty Celtic. With just a few minutes to go, they were leading 2–1, when A. Craig, their half back, headed through his own goal to level the scores at 2–2. The replay went to Celtic 4–2, and it took Motherwell four more finals and twenty-one more years before they finally won the Scottish Cup. Arsenal full back Dennis Evans put the ball past his own goalie in a League game in December 1955, thinking that a whistle from the crowd had been the referee's to end the game. He may not have been popular with his team-mates when the final whistle did at last blow, but at least he survived to tell the tale. When Andres Escobar, the Colombian captain, put through his own goal against the United States in the 1994 World Cup Finals, he may have guessed that it would mean his team's elimination from the competition. However, nobody could have suspected that just after taking an earlier than expected flight home, he would be shot dead in a Medellín car park on 2 July 1994, apparently by disgruntled football fans. Fortunately for Neil Carlstrom, the crime rate in Essex is lower – depending on whose statistics you believe – than in Colombia. Playing for Eton Manor against Canvey Island in the Essex Senior League in 1989–90, the defender managed to put through his own goal three times.

Of the six own goals scored in FA Cup Finals between 1877, when Wanderer Lord Kinnaird did it but still collected a winner's medal, and 1991, when Notts Forest's Des Walker was the guilty party, three have been cancelled out by the same player scoring for his own team as well. Bert Turner of Charlton Athletic put the ball past the long-suffering Sam Bartram in his own goal after eighty-five minutes of the 1946 Final, the first goal of a dour match. With only five minutes to go, things looked bleak for Charlton, but just one minute later Turner scored his only post-war goal for his team, to level the scores and force extra time. Unfortunately, Derby County scored three more goals in the extra half-hour, so Charlton lost the Cup. They were back at Wembley the next year, but by then Bert Turner had retired. His namesake but no relation, the amateur Arthur Turner, also played for Charlton in that match, and has the unique distinction of playing in the Cup Final for a team he never once represented in the League.

Tommy Hutchison of Manchester City scored both goals in the 1981 Final, first for his own team after twenty-nine minutes, and then the equalizer with twenty minutes to go. The match was still deadlocked after extra time, but Spurs won the replay five days later. Six years later, Coventry City and Tottenham Hotspur were locked at 2–2 as the ninety minutes ended, one of Spurs' goals coming from Gary Mabbutt. In extra time he clinched victory, but unfortunately it was victory for Coventry, thanks to Mabbutt's ninety-sixth-minute own goal. Mabbutt was playing in the Final five years later when Des Walker helped Spurs, rather than Notts Forest who were paying him, to win the Cup, and he was able to ruminate on the fact that nobody since Lord Kinnaird in the sixth year of the competition had scored an own goal in the Final and been on the winning side. But at least none of them has been assassinated.

Two players have scored two own goals in a League game,

but stopped would-be assassins in their tracks by also scoring two for their own side. Sam Wynne of Oldham Athletic at least had the compensation of ending up, appropriately, on the winning side, when they beat Manchester United 3–2 in a Second Division fixture on 6 October 1923. His goals for Oldham came from a free kick and a penalty. On the other hand, Chris Nicholl, the other four-goal hero and villain, playing for Aston Villa against Leicester City in the First Division on 20 March 1976, could only manage a 2–2 draw. Without him, it would have been a dull match indeed for the crowd of 24,663.

And 18,441 people would have been disappointed if Mike England and John Pratt had not combined to make the Spurs *v.* Burnley game on 5 October 1973 an exciting one. Both were playing for Spurs, but put through their own goals in the first half, making it 2–0 to the visitors. Either manager Terry Neill or goalkeeper Pat Jennings must have said something to them at half-time, for both then went out and scored at the correct end of the pitch. Indeed, Spurs would have secured a draw if Leighton James had not made it 3–2, with a shot that deflected off Mike England on its way past Jennings. England agreed not to claim a second own goal, even if it would have given him a hat-trick and a chance to keep the match ball.

Halifax Town's games were disappointing at the start of the 1990–1 season, and the crowds were thus considerably smaller than 18,441. Then on 5 October 1990, manager Jim McCalliog agreed an exchange deal with Carlisle manager Cliff Middlemass, which sent Halifax striker Tony Fyfe to Carlisle and Carlisle forward Steve Norris to Halifax. In seven League games up to that date, Halifax had not scored a single goal, and were bottom of the League. Norris, on the other hand, had already scored twice for Carlisle and was obviously what the Shaymen needed. In his first game for Halifax, against Scunthorpe, he failed to score, but a boring 0–0 draw was better than the six consecutive defeats that had preceded it. The next match was away to Carlisle, where both Norris and Fyfe faced their old team-mates. Halifax won 3–0 and Norris was one of the scorers. After that, there was no stopping him. Of Halifax's fifty-nine goals that season, Norris scored thirty, including eight penalties, and Halifax finished two places clear of the bottom of the League. For Carlisle, Tony Fyfe was less effective. They scored only thirty-seven more goals that season, averaging less than a goal a game, and they slipped from fifteenth to twentieth. Fyfe did not score for them until 27 April 1991, four games from the end of the season.

As there have been almost half a million goals scored in the Football League in the past one hundred years and more, not to mention many times that number in other professional, amateur, school and more or less friendly games around the world, it is not surprising that some of them have been controversial. In the 1932 Cup Final, Arsenal were 1–0 up when, in the thirty-eighth minute, Boyd of Newcastle took the ball to the goal line and crossed to Allen, who shot the ball into the net. The Arsenal players let the referee know that they thought the ball had been out of play before Boyd crossed it, and photographs published in the newspapers the next day showed they were right. The ball was over the goal line before the cross was made. Newcastle scored again in the second half – Allen again – and won the Cup. The next season Arsenal lost 2–0 at home to Walsall in the third round, perhaps the most devastating upset in Cup history.

Bob Kelly, a forward who played 522 games in the First Division for Burnley, Sunderland and Huddersfield in the 1920s, scored one of the odder goals of a championship season during Burnley's climb from the bottom of the table on 4 September 1920 to the top on 20 November 1920, where they stayed for the rest of the season. In one game the 'Burnley Flyer' hit such a powerful shot that his toecap came off his boot. The goalkeeper caught the toecap, but let the ball fly past him into the net. When Everton played Hull City in an FA Cup fourth-round replay on 2 February 1927 at Villa Park, the score was 2–2 and looking very much as though it would go to a third replay, when Scott of Hull shot the ball so hard that it burst as it went into the net. The goal stood and Hull won 3–2.

Probably the weakest shot on record was in a Dundee junior League game between the wars, when a forward slipped in the muddy penalty area as he rushed forward to tap the ball into an empty goal. His face being now rather nearer the ball than his feet or any of the opposing team were, he picked the heavy leather ball up in his teeth by the laces and crawled over the line. The goal was allowed.

The easiest goal ever scored in a top game was by Vale of

Leven, to win the 1879 Scottish Cup Final. After a 1–1 draw with Glasgow Rangers, a replay was called for, but Rangers refused to play. In order to win the Cup, Vale of Leven took the field, kicked off and ran the ball through an empty goal. Seventeen years later, in the English Amateur Cup Final between the Old Carthusians and the Casuals, the Old Carthusians may have feared that there was to be a repeat of the Rangers absentee policy. Several of the Casuals were late arriving at the ground, and one, L.V. Lodge, their left back, was so casual that he missed his train to the ground altogether. By the time he arrived, the match had kicked off and his team was winning 1–0. From then on, things went badly wrong and the Old Carthusians scored twice to secure victory. Lodge had arrived late, lost the match and not even had the consolation of seeing his own side score. Such is football.

## EXTRA TIME

*More goals than games*
Pelé, 1,000 goals in 909 games, 1956–69 (Pelé ended his career with 1,279 goals from 1,363 games)

Franz Binder, 1,006 goals in 756 games in Austria and Germany, 1930–50

Jimmy McGrory, 410 goals in 408 games for Celtic, 1922–38

Ferenc Puskas, 85 goals in 84 games for Hungary, 1945–56

Gerd Müller, 68 goals in 62 games for West Germany, 1966–74

Jim Smith, 66 goals in 38 games for Ayr United, 1927–8

Dixie Dean, 60 goals in 39 games for Everton, 1927–8

*Goal-shy away from home*

Alan Gilzean, Tottenham Hotspur, scored 26 goals in home games between February 1965 and October 1966, but none away from home. He went for 6 years and 14 days (9 January 1965 to 23 January 1971) without scoring a goal away from home in the FA Cup.

*Late comebacks include*

Old Etonians 5, Darwen 5 – FA Cup 4th round, 13 February 1879. Darwen were 5–1 down with 15 minutes to go.

Sunderland 5, Liverpool 5 – First Division, 19 January 1907. Liverpool were 4–1 up at half-time.

Fulham 3, Southampton 3 – Second Division, 3 November 1934. Southampton were 3–0 up with 8 minutes to go. All three goals were scored by Syd Gibbons, a defender.

Chelsea 2, Preston North End 1, FA Cup 4th round replay, 3 February 1969. The score after 89 minutes was 0–0. PNE scored in the final minute, then Chelsea scored two in time added on for injuries.

Hull City 4, Sheffield Wednesday 4 – Second Division, 26 December 1970. Hull were 4–1 up with 8 minutes to go.

QPR 5, Newcastle 5 – First Division, 22 September 1984. Newcastle were 4–0 up at half-time.

Portsmouth 4, Fulham 4, Second Division, 1 January 1985. Portsmouth were 4–0 up at half-time.

Leeds 4, Liverpool 5 – First Division, 13 April 1991. Liverpool were 4–0 up at half-time.

Birmingham City 4, Swindon Town 6 – First Division, 12 April 1993. Swindon were 4–1 down with 30 minutes to go.

Aston Villa 4, Leicester City 4 – Premiership, 22 February 1995. Aston Villa were 4–1 up with 13 minutes to go.

Walsall 8, Torquay 4 – FA Cup 1st round replay, 12 December 1995. Walsall scored 4 goals in 8 minutes of extra time.

Barnsley 3, Ipswich 3 – First Division, 9 March 1996. Barnsley were 3–0 up with 5 minutes to go.

*Quick goals*
3.5 seconds – Colin Cowperthwaite, Barrow *v.* Kettering Town, 8 December 1979
3.69 seconds – Damien Mori, Adelaide City *v.* Sydney United, 6 December 1995
4 seconds – Jim Fryatt, Bradford *v.* Tranmere Rovers, 25 April 1964
6 seconds – Pat Kruse (own goal) Torquay *v.* Cambridge United, 3 January 1977
7 seconds – Bob Langton, Preston North End *v.* Manchester City, First Division, 25 August 1948
8 seconds – Vic Lambden, Bristol Rovers *v.* Aldershot, FA Cup 3rd round, 10 January 1951
10 seconds – James Quinn, Blackpool *v.* Bristol Rovers, Second Division, 12 August 1995. The first goal of a new season.
10 seconds – Sammy Collins, Torquay *v.* Walsall, Third Division (South), August 1956. The fastest League penalty ever.
27 seconds – Bryan Robson, England *v.* France, Bilbao, 16 June 1982
40 seconds – Bob Chatt, Aston Villa *v.* WBA, FA Cup Final, 20 April 1895
45 seconds – Jackie Milburn, Newcastle United *v.* Manchester City, FA Cup Final, 7 May 1955

*Sixteen goals in a top-class match*
Stephan Stanis, Racing Club de Lens *v.* Aubry-Asturies, French Cup, 13 December 1942

*Thirteen goals in a Scottish Cup match*
John Petrie, Arbroath *v.* Bon Accord, 5 September 1885

*Ten goals in a League match*
Joe Payne, Luton Town *v.* Bristol Rovers, 13 April 1936

*Ten goals in an FA Cup match*
C. Marron, South Shields *v.* Radcliffe, 26 September 1947

*Nine goals in a League match*
'Bunny' Bell, Tranmere Rovers *v.* Oldham Athletic, 26 December 1935

*Nine goals in a Cup match*
E. MacDougall, Bournemouth *v.* Margate, 20 November 1971

*Eight goals in a Cup match*
J.D. Ross, Preston North End *v.* Hyde, 15 October 1887. Ross also twice scored six goals in Cup games.

*Eight goals in a Scottish League match*
O. McNally, Arthurlie *v.* Armadale, 1 October 1927
J. McGrory, Celtic *v.* Dunfermline Athletic, 14 September 1928
J. Dyet, King's Park *v.* Forfar Athletic, 2 January 1930
J. Calder, Morton *v.* Raith Rovers, 18 April 1936
N. Hayward, Raith Rovers *v.* Brechin City, 20 August 1937

*Seven goals in a League match*
J.D. Ross, Preston North End *v.* Stoke, 6 October 1888
A. Whitehurst, Bradford City *v.* Tranmere Rovers, 6 March 1929
E. Drake, Arsenal *v.* Aston Villa, 14 December 1935
E. Harston, Mansfield Town *v.* Hartlepool United, 23 January 1937
E. Gemmell, Oldham Athletic *v.* Chester, 19 January 1952
T. Briggs, Blackburn Rovers *v.* Bristol Rovers, 5 February 1955
N. Coleman, Stoke City *v.* Lincoln City, 23 February 1957

*Seven goals in a Cup match, and still on the losing side*
W. Minter, St Albans City *v.* Dulwich Hamlet, November 1922. St Albans lost 8–7.

*Six goals in twenty-one minutes*
F. Keetley, Lincoln City *v.* Halifax Town, 16 January 1932

*Four goals in five minutes*
J. McIntyre, Blackburn Rovers *v.* Everton, 16 September 1922
W. Richardson, West Bromwich Albion *v.* West Ham United, 7 November 1931

*Four goals in seven minutes*
F. Smith, Grimsby Town *v.* Hartlepools United, 15 November 1952

*Three goals in two and a half minutes*
J. Scarth, Gillingham *v.* Leyton Orient, 1 November 1952
*Three goals in first seven minutes of début*
E. Harston, Mansfield Town *v.* Southport, at Southport, 19 October 1935. The match ended in a 3–3 draw.

*Goal in first minute of début*
Ernie Shepherd, Hull City *v.* Darlington, March 1949
Bernard Evans, Wrexham, August 1954
Peter Ward, Brighton and Hove Albion, March 1976

*Thirteen goals in a Cup replay*
Tottenham Hotspur 13, Crewe Alexandra 2, 3 February 1960,
after a 2–2 draw at Crewe

*Sixteen goals in four games against the same opponents*
V. Watson, West Ham United *v.* Leeds United, 6 goals on 9
February 1929, 3 on 16 November 1929, 4 on 25 January 1930,
3 on 21 March 1931

*Goal disallowed because referee blew for full time as the ball was*
*flying into the net*
Crystal Palace *v.* Portsmouth, 23 March 1996. A shot by Andy
Roberts of Crystal Palace hit the back of the net just after the
whistle. The final score was 0–0.
Brazil *v.* Sweden, World Cup 1978, in Argentina. Zico headed in a
late corner to break a 1–1 deadlock, but referee Clive Thomas
had already blown the final whistle.

*Goal scored with the head from 35 yards out*
David Moss, Luton *v.* Queen's Park Rangers, 8 November 1980

*Goal disallowed because it went in off a mongrel using the*
*goalpost as urinal*
Tony Hunt, Brampton Dynamos, 1989–90

*Hat-trick scored past three different goalkeepers*
David Herd, Manchester United *v.* Sunderland, 26 November
1966. Herd scored four, past Jim Montgomery, Charlie Hurley
and John Parke.
Chris Pike, Hereford United *v.* Colchester, 16 October 1993. Pike
scored three including a penalty. The first two goalies, John
Keeley and Mickey Desborough were both sent off.

# COME OFF IT, REF!

## 5

The most significant thing about a game that is bound by rules (in football's case, they are called laws, and there are just seventeen of them) is that the participants spend much of their time working out ways of getting round them. When the 1992 back pass law was enacted, preventing the goal-keeper from picking up a ball passed back to him by one of his own team, German players quickly found a way to exploit the loophole that allowed the goalie to handle a back pass made with any other part of the body than the foot. In the very first games played under the new law, defenders were going down on their knees to prod the ball back with their thighs, or to head it along the ground to the man in the brightly coloured jersey. Brentford goalie Kevin Dearden thought he had worked out a way with defender Martin Grainger to overcome the back pass law, so when they were awarded a free kick just outside their own penalty area in the match against Burnley on 3 February 1996, Grainger passed the ball to his goalie, who was standing next to him. Dearden then dribbled the ball back to the box and picked it up to boot it upfield. The referee, Alan Wiley of Walsall, knew his laws better than the Brentford defence and immediately awarded Burnley a free kick, from which they almost scored. Other teams will no doubt try to think of more ways round this law, and any others that may be introduced in seasons to come.

The referee has to know his rule book, or else diplomatic incidents can arise. He has, for example, to know the proper dimensions of the goal. On 15 November 1989, a Youth International between England and Czechoslovakia was scheduled at Portsmouth's ground, Fratton Park. The Danish referee, Jan Dangaard, checked the height of the crossbar on one of the goals, and discovered that it was about one inch too low. He ordered the bar to be raised, much to the embarrassment of the Portsmouth groundstaff, who had already overseen nine League games that season. England won the international 1–0, and Portsmouth, with the right-sized goals, went on to enjoy much better fortune. Having won only two of their first nine games, they then won seven of the remaining fourteen at Fratton Park, and the average number of goals per game rose from three to 3.4. It's amazing what that extra inch could do. Six years later, a local club in Honiton, Devon, had trouble scoring until it was discovered that their crossbars were a full six inches too low, while in Spain, Third Division Castellon realized rather belatedly that their crossbars were even lower, about eight inches below the regulation height. Oddly, this 8 per cent reduction in target area resulted in a 50 per cent difference in the number of goals that Castellon scored at home compared with their away strike rate (eight at home, twelve away).

85

Not all referees are as aware of the laws as Mr Dangaard. When Ecuador played Venezuela in the Olympic qualifying tournament in Mar del Plata, Argentina, at the beginning of 1996, the referee awarded a penalty to Ecuador. This in itself was a daring decision, but greater foolhardiness was to follow. The Ecuador defender Matamba stepped up and blasted the ball into the back of the net. 'Goal!' shouted the Ecuador team and all its fans. 'No goal!' shouted the Venezuelans, who

pointed out that as Matamba kicked the ball, his boot had flown off and also rocketed into the back of the net. The referee thought about it for a while, and then ordered the penalty to be retaken. Matamba stepped up again, kicked again and his boot flew off again. This time it hit a post and the ball hit the crossbar. No goal. The Ecuador team were incensed but played on, eventually losing 5–2 and rendering any dispute about the penalty academic. Academic dispute is obviously a popular pastime in Ecuador, however, because the press corps immediately consulted the FIFA officials, who agreed that there was no law covering the loss of a boot in mid-kick, and that the first penalty kick should have been allowed. They also suggested that Matamba keep his boots more securely tied in future.

The referee's problems are not confined to subtle bending of the rules by players who have attempted to study the letter of the law. The biggest problem concerns unruly behaviour. Red and yellow cards are these days more frequent than goals, and at some grounds more numerous than spectators. In a local cup match between Tongham Youth Club and Hawley, at Tongham in Surrey on 3 November 1969, the referee John McAdam booked all twenty-two players, including one who was taken to hospital. He followed this up by booking one of the linesmen for dissent. Tongham won 2–0 and, as one of the winning team said, 'It was a good hard game.'

This feat was repeated in the 1990–1 season, when Dr John Gayford, a psychiatrist by trade but a referee by inclination, took charge of the crucial Croydon Municipal Officers Reserves *v.* Merton Municipal Officers Reserves at Croydon, and put all the players' names in his book. Perhaps Dr Gayford remembered the precedent set by Michael Woodhams, who sent off one entire team and several of its officials in a game at Waltham Abbey in Essex two days before Christmas 1973. The offending team was called Juventus-Cross, but its opponents would have had a great problem scoring goals once they had the pitch to themselves, simply because they would be permanently offside. The same problem would have faced the players of Toledo Imperial of Spain in their game against Gamonal in the 1990–1 season. The referee sent off the entire Gamonal team, stating only that 'I was insulted gravely.' This was the same complaint made by a Mr Tarbet of Bearsden in a Scottish local League game between Glencraig United and Goldenhill Boys' Club on 2 February 1975. Mr Tarbet had officiated at games involving Glencraig before, and the team remembered him well – so well indeed that on his arrival he was greeted with a raucous chanting from the Glencraig dressing room. Mr Tarbet took exception to the lyrics of the song that was echoing around the dressing rooms and booked the entire Glencraig side even before they had got out on to the pitch for the pre-match warm-up. For the record, the game ended in a 2–2 draw.

On 1 June 1993, in the Paraguayan winter, the League

87

match between General Caballero and Sportivo Ameliano
ended in chaos after referee William Weiler was forced to send
off two players for fighting. This decision provoked a ten-
minute fight involving all the remaining players. Weiler sorted
it out by sending off a further eighteen players, including the
rest of the Sportivo Ameliano team. The only two players left
were on the General Caballero side, but the game could not
continue with only two participants, so it was abandoned.

88 In an Eastern Counties League match at Wisbech,
Cambridgeshire, in October 1973, the visiting team Yarmouth
was four goals up with twenty minutes left to play. The referee, David Jessup, had had to book six players during the
course of the game, but at this point fighting broke out on
the pitch. Mr Jessup ordered both teams to the dressing
rooms, but subsequently abandoned the game. 'I took the
players off for a cooling-off period,' he said, 'but I didn't consider it safe for the players or officials to return to the pitch.'
Up to 1973 Wisbech had never been high on the list of towns
where crowd passions ran high and footballing violence was
rife, but the man in black obviously sensed that the mood
was turning ugly.

His action did not officially constitute sending off all twenty-two players. It was left to Rochdale, birthplace of the Co-operative Movement, to play host to the most disreputable game of all time. On 25 February 1951, Lily Mills FC faced the Ukrainian Sports Club of Rochdale in a key fixture. The game quickly degenerated into a hopeless brawl, so the referee sent off all the participants. Even this did not stop the fracas, so he set about cautioning those members of the crowd who joined in the fun. How he managed to get away from Rochdale in one piece is not recorded. Slightly less draconian was Oscar Roberto de Godoi, refereeing the Corinthians *v.* São Paolo match in Brazil in March 1995. He sent off a mere four players and booked only twelve, all in a ten-minute period late in the first half. At half-time the players of both sides, convinced that their official was drunk, insisted on a blood test.

89

If a referee cannot send off all the team at one time, he can perhaps gain equal satisfaction from sending off one of the team all the time. Nigel Pepper, the York City midfield player, had a bad time against Darlington in the 1990–1 season. By the time the two teams had met for the fifth time that season (two League games, two FA Cup games and a Leyland Daf Trophy meeting), Pepper had been sent off in three of the games, surviving the full ninety minutes only twice. Despite their lack of numbers, thanks to Pepper's determination to get into the bath well before his team-mates, York lost only one of the five games, won two and drew the other two.

Referees have always to be on the lookout for illegal play. This is not just a matter of knowing when a defender has tapped a forward's ankles, or whether a handball was deliberate. It is a question of keeping a wary eye out for odd trends during play, which imply that all is not being played strictly according to the rules. For example, during a deaf-and-dumb League match in Turkey in 1989, a jubilant goal scorer yelled, 'Goal!' (in Turkish, of course), leading vigilant officials to believe that the player was not all he was supposed to be, namely deaf and dumb. The match was awarded to the other side.

Paul Gascoigne was once booked for booking the referee. When Dougie Smith dropped his yellow card in the Rangers *v.* Hibernian Scottish Premier Division game at Ibrox Park on 30 December 1995, Gazza picked it up and waved it at the ref, who, showing a great sense of humour, promptly booked Gazza. Alan Shearer of Blackburn Rovers was booked in a Premiership match in the previous season for 'imitating a linesman', while Ruben Oliveira, of Santo in the Uruguayan First Division, was sent off in 1990–1 for kissing an opponent who had missed an easy goal. Ataulfo Valencia, playing for the Ecuadorian team Espoli against a team called Barcelona (but not the Spanish one) in the South American Cup, was shown the red card for punching the driver of a trolley sent onto the field to remove an injured player. The trolley had driven into Valencia and knocked him over, so he might well have had to leave the field injured, even had he not been sent off.

Damien Webber of Millwall managed to get himself into the record books in only his third full League appearance, which turned out not to be a full appearance after all. He became the first man to be booked by one referee and sent off by another in the same League match for fouling the same man twice. On 14 January 1995, Millwall were away to Sheffield United in the Second Division, and after thirty-four minutes Webber fouled the United winger Andy Scott. Referee Paul Harrison duly booked him and eleven minutes later blew his whistle for half-time. During the interval, the ref was taken ill and the second half began with Ken Powell in charge. Only two minutes later, Webber was deemed to have fouled Scott again, and this time he got the red card. Webber was philosophical, as merits a man who began his career with Diadora League strugglers Bognor Regis Town. 'I knew when Scott tripped over my foot early in the second half I would probably have to go. My only hope was that the refs hadn't exchanged notes at half-time.' Mr Harrison had not been as ill as that.

91

Two referees in a game is not a normal occurrence, but it does happen from time to time when one official gets injured or ill during the game. Jimmy Hill, a registered referee, once ran the line at a Coventry game when the linesman pulled a muscle and there was no replacement to be found outside the directors' box. But to have two referees on purpose is much more curious. Following reports of a similar test in Czechoslovakia, the Football Association sanctioned an experiment in two international trials in 1935, using Dr A.W. Barton, a public schoolmaster, and Mr E. Wood, who had refereed the 1933 Cup Final, in both games. The games proved

the foolishness of using two referees to control one game, but in a Spennymoor Sunday League Cup match in County Durham sixty years later, they decided to give the idea another go. Spennymoor Voltigeur were playing Highland Laddie (where do they get these names from?), and Jimmy Handley refereed one half of the pitch while Gordon McMillan controlled the other half. The game went reasonably well, but there was a distinct difference in the level of discipline prevailing in each half. Handley booked four players, but McMillan kept a clean sheet. A fellow referee described the experiment as 'completely wrong – one of those things that makes you shudder just to think about it.'

Football can produce all sorts of things to make you shudder, most of them far worse than the spectre of two referees. Eric Cantona's celebrated flying kick at a spectator – one hesitates to use the word 'fan' – during Manchester United's game against Crystal Palace on 25 January 1995 is one such, but this extraordinary act of precision violence was more terrible in retrospect than it was at the time. At the time it was just funny. In retrospect, we see what would have been the full implications of not punishing such an act: for a start, Manchester United would probably have done the double again that season, if Cantona had been available to play for them all year, and how boring that would have been for the majority (just) of the population of England who are not Manchester United fans. Crystal Palace still went down at the end of the season, with or without their vocal accompaniment.

On 3 April 1915, in a League game towards the end of the only official football season ever played during wartime, an act of subversion took place with a long-term impact potentially greater than even Eric the Terrible's. William Cook, Oldham Athletic's full back, committed a foul in the fifty-fifth minute of the League match against Middlesbrough at Ayresome Park, and was sent off. Or at least the referee told him to go, but Cook had other ideas. He swore at the referee, sat down in the middle of the pitch and refused to move. At the time Oldham were 4–1 down to Middlesbrough, and Cook's action may not have been taken merely because he was upset at this particular decision. Oldham were top of the First Division table, with only a handful of games left to play and a game in hand over their closest challengers, and perhaps Cook that thought by getting the game abandoned, Oldham could start again another day and change the result. If that was his plan, it misfired. The match was indeed abandoned, but the League insisted that the result stand. Oldham went on to gain only six points from their remaining six games, even though four of them were at home, while their nearest rivals Everton, who had only one home fixture left, took nine points from their final five games, to win the title by one point from the despairing Oldham. Oldham have never won the League Championship and can put the blame for their failure in 1915 at the door of William Cook. Perhaps that was his true punishment, because it took the Football League another eight months before they banned Cook from football, by which time the war had led to the curtailment of all Football League games anyway. When the war ended and the Football League put out one of its first representative teams of the post-war era, to play against the Irish League in November 1919, the left back position was filled by one W. Cook (Oldham Athletic).

By an odd coincidence, in the final season before the next war, a different William Cook played full back for Everton, the team that took the title from Oldham in 1915. His particular claim to fame was the unlikely feat of scoring from the penalty spot in three consecutive games in four days: against Blackpool on Christmas Eve 1938, against Derby County on Boxing Day at Goodison Park, and the very next day in the return game at Derby's Baseball Ground.

The year 1914–15 was a bad one for the Football League. The Middlesbrough *v.* Oldham match took place one day after the infamous Manchester United *v.* Liverpool match, which was won 2–0 by Manchester United. This match was fixed.

The official explanation was that several of the players were convinced that football would be discontinued during the war and that by betting on the correct scoreline they would make plenty of money at a difficult time, at the expense of the book-makers. The fact that Manchester United would have been relegated, had they not won the game, was purely incidental. One of the players involved, the Manchester United forward E.J. West, sued the Football Association and the *Athletic News* for libel, but lost his case and then admitted the charge. Eight players were subsequently banned for life, but Manchester United stayed in the top division until 1922, when relegation was unavoidable.

Sending players off is an occupational hazard for referees, and one that sometimes does not achieve the desired result. Kenny Low was refereeing an East of Scotland League game between Easthouses Lily and Civil Service Strollers in November 1995, when he sent off Easthouses' John Neilson. Once back in the changing rooms, Neilson made his way to the referee's room, found Low's socks and exacted his revenge by cutting them in half. Four months later he was banned by the Scottish FA for eighteen months, rather longer than the punishment meted out to Eric Cantona. Obviously a referee's socks are more precious than Crystal Palace fans.

It was also in Scotland that a dismissed player in an

Edinburgh amateur game in 1994 climbed into his car and, while the game was still in progress, drove it straight across the pitch at the referee. He missed, unlike Livingston Thistle goalkeeper Alan Sneddon in their game against Stirling University. Sneddon rushed out of his goal with the admirable intention of stopping a scuffle that was developing between two players, but one of the fighting duo took exception to the peacemaker, calling him fat. Sneddon was not amused and smashed the Stirling player in the mouth, knocking out two of his teeth. Sneddon's next fixture was with Stirling Sheriff's Court, where he was fined £200 for assault. 'It is meant to be a game,' said Sheriff Angela Bowman, who has obviously never heard of Bill Shankly.

In the Scottish Mr Shankly's spiritual home of Birkenhead, magistrates heard that Kenneth John Croft, thirty-one, took exception to the retaking of a penalty that levelled the scores in an amateur game in which he was playing in late 1972. Rather than merely grit his teeth and get on with trying to win the game, Croft strode over to the referee and knocked him unconscious, so the game had to be abandoned as a draw. Croft was fined £40 with £20 costs, and bound over for a year, not to incapacitate any more referees until 1974.

Teeth can be a problem for referees. Henning Erikstrup was in charge of the Noerager *v.* Ebeltoft match in Denmark in April 1960, and Noerager were winning 4–3 as Erikstrup prepared to blow the final whistle. Unfortunately at this moment his false teeth fell out. Rather than risk a gummy blow on the whistle, Erikstrup bent down to recover his teeth, but while he was doing so Ebeltoft scored an equalizer. Erikstrup disallowed the goal and blew for full time, but Ebeltoft, naturally enough, appealed to the Jutland football authorities. They claimed that the final whistle had not been blown when Ebeltoft equalized, so the goal should stand. Erikstrup argued that he had not actually blown for full time, but the ninety minutes were up and 'I had to get my teeth back before some player put his big foot on them.'

When Burnley played Blackburn Rovers on 12 December 1891, the weather was foul. The snow was coming down and at half-time Burnley were 3–0 up. After half-time, with the weather still terrible, only seven of the Blackburn players re-emerged from the comparative warmth of the dressing rooms. The referee, Charles Clegg, a no-nonsense official who was to referee that season's Cup Final, insisted that the remaining players come out, but within a very short while disagreements had broken out, and Clegg was forced to send off Joe Lofthouse, the Blackburn and England winger, and Yates, the Burnley captain. At this, all the remaining Blackburn players apart from Herby Arthur, their goalkeeper, headed for the great indoors with Lofthouse. Clegg insisted that the game continue, and Nichol of Burnley scored a fourth goal, one of the easiest of his career. However, Arthur in goal successfully appealed for offside, but then refused to take the resulting free kick. At this point, with the snow lying deep (and probably anything but crisp and even) on the pitch, even Clegg had to admit defeat. The match was abandoned and awarded to Burnley, 3–0. The weather was obviously dreadful in Lancashire that day, as just down the road at Deepdale, the game between Preston North End and Notts County was abandoned when six Notts County players, 6–0 down at the time, gave up the unequal struggle and marched off.

You have to get the right man to send off, of course. Otherwise they will look all hurt and innocent, like Middlesbrough's Terry Cooper when he was sent off at Chelsea on 22 March 1975 for remarks he had made to the linesman. 'I thought the referee was pointing to a plane in the sky when he sent me off,' said the aggrieved Cooper. He could not have been as aggrieved as Zaire's Mulamba Ndaie, who was dismissed for kicking the referee in the international against Yugoslavia in the 1974 World Cup. Ndaie was not the culprit; it was his team-mate Ilunga Mwepu. Have sympathy, too, for Southampton's Danny Wallace, sent off in the game against Newcastle United on 14 December 1985. Jimmy Case committed a foul, but referee David Allison booked Wallace for the offence by mistake. Later in the game Wallace was booked again, this time correctly, but a second booking meant that he was sent off. Southampton went on to lose 2–1, but Wallace appealed against his booking, which video evidence proved was indeed a mistake. The referee really should have got it right first time, as Case is five foot nine inches tall and weighs twelve and a half stone – five inches taller than Wallace and two and a half stone heavier. Oh, and Case is white but Wallace is black.

Video evidence is not always totally reliable, though. When Edmundo of Corinthians in Brazil struck a Santos defender and was sent off during the 1995–6 season, he hoped that video evidence would exonerate him at the subsequent hearing. Unfortunately, the Corinthians' officials brought the wrong tape to the hearing and treated the disciplinary committee to half an hour of the adventures of the television cartoon dog Scooby Doo. Scooby Doo has agreed never to play Brazilian League football again.

Footballers are not the only people who cause trouble. John McLoughlin of Poplar, East London, claims to be the only ball boy to be sent off in a League game. The game was at Somerton Park, a Third Division (South) match between Newport County and Notts County on 8 October 1949. Somerton Park in those days had a greyhound track around the pitch, so six ball boys were needed, two on each side and one at each end, to recover the ball when it was hit into touch but not as far as the crowd. The ball boys wore white shirts and black shorts, which were the same colours that the visitors wore. After about ten minutes, the great Tommy Lawton, newly signed by Notts County, complained to the referee that the Notts players were confused by the six extra players in black and white around the edges of the field, so the referee came over to McLoughlin, the nearest ball boy to the action, and told him and his colleagues to go off and change into something less confusing. This is the only recorded case of a ball boy being dismissed in a League game. Ball boys have threatened to strike, though. They were so upset by the lack of soft drinks during the early season games at Clyde that they said they would not turn up for duty at the game against East Fife on 12 November 1994 unless there was more for them to drink. Eventually an embarrassing clash was averted, and the fully refreshed ball boys performed as usual, as Clyde pottered unspectacularly along to a 1–1 draw in front of 1,212 faithful spectators.

Football remains a friendly game, however much players and the authorities may clash. When Folkestone Invicta defender Dave Ward was sent off in a Winstonlead Kent First Division game against Dartford in 1995, he compounded his offence by getting involved in a fight with a Dartford supporter as he left the field. Ward was sacked by Folkestone for the offence, and at the subsequent Kent FA disciplinary hearing he was banned from all football until 31 December 1996. Given his record of being sent off five times and sacked by two different clubs, he was lucky to escape so lightly. Folkestone Invicta manager Tim Hulme was quoted as saying that 'The sentence reflects the seriousness of the offence. The committee has acted in the best interests of the game. But I have to take this opportunity to say that Dave is a very nice bloke and he will always be welcome at Folkestone.' So that's all right, then.

## EXTRA TIME

*Father and son refereeing Cup Finals*
Arthur Kingscott refereed the 1900 and 1901 Finals; Harry
Kingscott refereed in 1931.

*Referee in Cup Final after winning Cup winner's medal*
Charles Alcock refereed the Finals of 1875 and 1879, having won
the Cup as part of the Wanderers team in 1872.
W.S. Rawson refereed the Final of 1876, having won the Cup as
part of the Oxford University team of 1874.

*Referee in Cup Final after winning Cup runner's-up medal*
Major F. Marindin, Royal Engineers, was a finalist in 1872 and
1874, and refereed the Finals of 1880, 1883 and 1885–90
inclusive.

*Referee in at least three Cup Finals*
8 – Major F. Marindin, 1880, 1883, 1885, 1886, 1887, 1888,
1889 and 1890
3 – C.W. Alcock, 1875, 1875 replay, 1879
3 – C.J. Hughes, 1891, 1893, 1894
3 – A. Kingscott, 1900, 1901, 1901 replay
3 – J. Lewis, 1895, 1897, 1898
3 – A. Stair, 1872, 1873, 1874

*Cup Final referees subsequently knighted*
J.C. Clegg (1882 and 1892), afterwards Sir Charles Clegg
Major F. Marindin (1880, 1883, 1885–90), afterwards Sir Francis
Marindin
S.F. Rous (1934), afterwards Sir Stanley Rous

*Referees who became League managers*
Herbert Bamlett (Manchester United, 1927–31)
Albert Prince-Cox (Bristol Rovers, 1930–6)
Jimmy Jewell (Norwich City, 1939)

*Referee blows for time ten minutes early by mistake*
Millwall *v.* Southampton at the Den, Southern League, November
1898. The referee at fault was Mr Saywell. The game was
completed five months later. Southampton won 4–1.

*Players cautioned for fighting with own team-mate*
H. Hay & J. Symington, Stranraer, 1974–5
Mike Flanagan & Derek Hales, Charlton Athletic *v.* Maidstone

United, 9 January 1979
Eric Steele & Gary Williams, Brighton *v.* Manchester United, 6
October 1979
Tony Rees & Tom Watson, Grimsby Town *v.* Darlington, 11
December 1990
Craig Levein & Graeme Hogg, Hearts pre-season friendly,
1994–5
David Batty & Graeme Le Saux, Blackburn Rovers *v.* Spartak
Moscow, 22 November 1995

*Player booked after five seconds*
Vinnie Jones, Sheffield United *v.* Manchester City, 19 January
1991, by ref David Elleray

*Player shown red card eats it*
Fernando D'Ercoli, Pianta *v.* Arpax, Italian amateur League game,
1989–90

*Player booked for making sign of the cross*
Rod McDonald (Partick Thistle) was banned for three games in
March 1996 after crossing himself in a game against Rangers. It
was deemed to be an 'inflammatory gesture'. Later in the game
McDonald was booked again by referee Jim McGilvray and
sent off.

*Both goalkeepers sent off for swearing at own side*
Langley Park *v.* Northallerton, Northern League Second Division,
1989–90. Referee Colin Revel. The match ended 0–0.

*Club withdraws from FA Cup after three players sent off*
Staines *v.* Dunstable, 1989–90. Dunstable had three men sent off,
the remaining eight walked off and the club withdrew from the
competition in protest.

*Match abandoned because of bad language*
Fleur-de-Lys *v.* Abertillery Town, 1995, abandoned after 70
minutes because of general use of foul language. Ref Roy
Meadows and linesman Bill Edwards could take no more.

*International goal set up by referee*
Norway 2, England 0, Under-21 International, 13 October 1992.
Norway's first goal, scored by Strandli, came to his feet after it
bounced off the referee.

# THAT'S ENTERTAINMENT

## 6

Football is entertainment. That applies equally whether you are standing in the rain, watching a dour end-of-season struggle between two teams in the middle of the Second Division table, or sitting comfortably at home with a can of beer in one hand and the remote control in the other, flicking between the European football on one channel and the Premiership highlights on another. Football is a sport, and sport is entertainment.

It is therefore no real surprise that the worlds of sport and the arts come together most closely over the football pitch. Entertainment for the fans who turn up to see the game is not limited to the football itself. Many other ways of keeping them amused have been tried over the years, from athletics, greyhound racing and magic displays to community singing and, of course, match announcements over the loudspeaker system. Where once they just used to announce the team line-up, these days announcers have turned the Tannoy into a mouthpiece for all types of odd items. At Bristol Rovers, in their local derby with City on 26 January 1991, the announcer Keith Valle told the crowd of a substitution in the City line-up with the words, 'Here comes their sub, Junior Bent. I'll bet he is.' Valle was soon looking for other employment. At Watford, in a game against Newcastle at Vicarage Road on 9 March 1991, they tried broadcasting the cheering crowd over the loudspeaker, like canned laughter in a television sitcom. It did no good; Watford still lost 2–1. At Newcastle United they have gone even further down the long and winding road towards weird entertainment, with the release of magpies into the crowd. At Newcastle's match against Manchester City in March 1996, a magpie was released, and this act of liberation featured on that evening's BBC *Match of the Day*. It provoked a flurry of letters to the BBC and an official complaint from the Royal Society for the Protection of Birds, which claimed that it was cruel to the magpie. What the Newcastle supporters who released the magpie clearly did not realize is that magpies are 'one for sorrow, two for joy'. If only they had released two magpies, things might have gone better. Within days, Newcastle's lead at the top of the Premiership, which had been so strong all season, had entirely disappeared.

103

Broadcasting and football first came together in Britain when BBC Radio broadcast a commentary on the First Division game between Arsenal and Sheffield United on 22

January 1927. It ended 1–1. Within ten years, the rights to the sights and sounds of the FA Cup Final were beginning to create commercial rivalry and skulduggery. In 1936, a dispute arose between the Wembley Stadium authorities and the news-reel companies, and on the day of the Final, 25 April, cameramen who had not been allowed to film from within the ground tried to hover overhead in aeroplanes and auto-gyros, their cameras trained on the action below. The Wembley authorities had been prepared for this, however, and had installed searchlights, which they shone at the aircraft in order to prevent them from filming the game. It ended 1–0 to Arsenal over Sheffield United, and it appears that there was no bootleg film of Ted Drake's winning goal in the seventy-fifth minute, or of any other part of the match. Since then, the squabbles between film and television companies over the rights to the Final have reached epic proportions, and even Parliament has felt the need to step in and ensure that the rights to such an important national event are retained for the nation at large.

Charlton Athletic's players and fans have mixed feelings about the value of television coverage. Their team went for 47 years and 285 days without winning a game shown live on television. They won the FA Cup Final on 26 April 1947, 1–0 after extra time against Burnley, but then had to wait until 5 February 1995 for their next televised success, once again 1–0, but this time in a First Division game against West Bromwich Albion.

Nowadays, the television record of every game has a value. Fans will buy videos of their team's games at the end of each season, although if you bought Portsmouth's video of the 1990–1 season, you will know that it turned out to be a video of Port Vale's games.

And television has tried to depict football on a fictional level, with programmes like *The Manageress*, written by Stan Hey and Andrew Nickolds and starring Cherie Lunghi and Warren Clarke, and *United!*, a football soap opera that ran for just over a year on BBC in 1965 and 1966. The former was entirely bearable, the latter was dreadful. Bruce Grobbelaar has appeared in a non-speaking cameo role in Channel Four's *Brookside*; and *Fantasy Football League*, a strange amalgam of comedy show, game show, chat show and car-boot sale, starring Frank Skinner and David Baddiel, has boosted BBC2's late-night ratings in the mid-1990s. It has also given hope to all those who thought that their impression of Jimmy Greaves was so bad that they could never earn money from it.

Films about football have generally not been much good, either artistically or football-wise. There is always the problem of actors looking too old or too unfit for the roles they are asked to play, and occasionally just too incompetent either to act or to play football. One of the best-known football films is the highly unlikely *Escape to Victory*, made in 1981, which told the story of a team of prisoners of war who are forced to play against the might of Hitler's German team, and who plot an escape through the team bathtub at half-time. The film starred Michael Caine (then aged forty-eight) and Sylvester Stallone. Despite being called *Escape to Victory*, the result of the match was actually 4–4, thanks to a last-minute penalty save by goalkeeper Stallone, who was obviously happier with a score draw than an outright win. Four years earlier, as 'Rocky', he had fought to a draw in his challenge for the world heavyweight championship, so this film brought up a unique celluloid double of draws that were billed as victories. Also starring in the film were the combined talents of the

Brazilian Pelé, the Argentinian Ossie Ardiles, England's Bobby Moore, the Pole Kasimiercz Deyna, Belgium's Paul van Himst, more Englishmen in Mike Summerbee and Russell Osman, and the Dutchman Co Prins. Where the Germans had been fighting in order to capture this particular motley band of prisoners of war was never revealed. Scotland's John Wark also featured in the film, and when it was shown on BBC Television on the afternoon of Sunday 3 March 1996, he achieved the

remarkable feat of being seen playing football in wartime Germany at exactly the same time as he was scoring for Ipswich Town in their 4–2 League victory over Leicester City. Wark even went so far as to miss a penalty in the seventy-fourth minute of that match, no doubt re-enacting the climax of the film in which he had been involved fifteen years earlier.

Football has been the subject of feature films since 1920, when *The Winning Goal* was made in England. Since then, films based on football have been made all round the world, with titles like *Comrade President*, *The Centre-Forward* (Yugoslavia, 1962), *Fish, Football and Girls* (Israel, 1968) and *Women Who Have Run Offside* (Czechoslovakia, 1951).

In 1939, the English director Thorold Dickinson made *The Arsenal Stadium Mystery*, a simple tale of intrigue and double-dealing set at Highbury, starring Leslie Banks and Greta Gynt as well as 'the players and management of Arsenal FC'. It was clearly a good fifty years ahead of its time. *Gregory's Girl* (1982), directed by Bill Forsyth and starring John Gordon Sinclair and Dee Hepburn, was one of the best of all the films with a football theme, while *Stubby*, a Swedish film made in 1974, which told the story of a six-year-old girl who becomes a professional football star, must rank as one of the silliest.

But however bad the films about football may have been, there is one art form to which football has made its own massive contribution, albeit definitely at the lower end of the scale. That art form is music, although when the two combine, the result is not always within the scope of even the broadest definition of music. Music and football seem to be as much a part of each other as a centre back's studs in a striker's kneecap, and football songs have reshaped the way people in Britain think about popular music. It used to be that when we thought of football and music, we thought of 'Abide With Me' sung dutifully and lustily before each Cup Final, and we always wondered why this particular hymn, with its singularly inappropriate words for a football match, should have become so closely associated with the FA Cup. The answer is that it was King George V's favourite hymn, and when he first visited a Cup Final, at Crystal Palace in 1914, the band played it in his honour. For the record, he and 72,777 others saw Burnley beat Liverpool 1–0. He also attended eight other finals, so by the time of his death in 1936 'Abide With Me' was firmly established as part of the Cup Final tradition.

There is a brief snatch on record of the 1932 Arsenal team singing 'Here We Go Again', but the first football 'pop' song

107

to achieve any popularity was recorded over a quarter of a century later. It was called 'Football Crazy', recorded by the Scottish folk duo Robin Hall and Jimmie MacGregor in 1960. Although it did not break through into the pop charts, it gained plenty of air-time and persuaded many record company executives that there was money to be made out of football, if only they could work out how. By the early 1960s several musicians who were football-crazy themselves were beginning to break through onto the bestseller lists, including former Brentford FC triallist Rod Stewart, and Reginald Dwight – cousin of Nottingham Forest's 1959 Cup Final goalscorer Roy Dwight – who now called himself Elton John. Thirty years on, every pop star seeking street-cred pledges his or her allegiance to one League team or other, whether it is 1990s Britpop heroes Oasis offering to sponsor Manchester City's kit or 1980s five-piece band Half Man Half Biscuit, who turned down appearances on television on Friday nights because they clashed with Tranmere Rovers home games.

The change in the relationship between pop music and football began when George Martin persuaded Gerry and the Pacemakers that their third single release, to follow up consecutive no. 1 hits with 'How Do You Do It' and 'I Like It', should be the lament from Rodgers and Hammerstein's 1945 Broadway musical *Carousel*. The song in question was called 'You'll Never Walk Alone', and its success ensured that Gerry and the Pacemakers became the first act in British recording history to take each of their first three singles to no. 1 in what was then known as the hit parade. Gerry Marsden and his Pacemakers were all from Liverpool, and their third chart-topper came in November 1963, at the start of a season that would end with Liverpool winning the League title for the first time in seventeen years – the beginning of a period of domination of the English game by one club that had never been seen before. For some reason, the Liverpool fans adopted the song that was hammered out over the Tannoy during the latter part of 1963, and they carried on singing it long after Gerry's version had dropped out of the charts. Before long it was a football anthem. Within a few years it had become *the* football anthem.

In retrospect, it took rather longer for football songs to hit the charts than we should have expected. Crowds took to singing, and adapting, the latest hits at every League ground in the country once Liverpool's Kop had shown them the way, but none of these wonderful renditions ever got as far as the recording studio. Then in 1970, in a move that can be seen to be as important to football as Manchester United's alternate kit policy, and as important to music as the invention of the Nolan Sisters, two Scotsmen came up with a song for the England World Cup squad to sing. That year in Mexico they were defending the trophy won in England four years earlier, and a theme song seemed the obvious way to encourage the

109

troops. The song, written by Bill Martin and Phil Coulter, who had already inflicted 'Puppet on a String' on an unsuspecting Eurovision public three years earlier, was called 'Back Home', and it soared all the way to the very top of the charts, despite the obvious fact that the squad's vocal talents were even more limited than their footballing ones. It gave Geoff Hurst the unique record of being the only county cricketer to top the charts, as the England striker had also played one county game for Essex (oddly enough, in Liverpool) a few seasons earlier.

From then on, there was no stopping the record industry. In 1971, Arsenal did the double and also hit no. 16 in the charts with the imaginatively titled 'Good Old Arsenal', with lyrics, astonishingly, by Jimmy Hill. Yes, that Jimmy Hill, who was at the time in limbo between his periods as manager and then director of Coventry City FC. It is good to know that he was able to make some sort of income from football at that difficult time, no doubt helped by the good vibrations emanating from Coventry City's reserve goalkeeper in 1971, David Icke. Hill's collaborator on this milestone in musical history was called Hunter, but we have it on good authority that it was not Norman 'Bite Yer Legs' Hunter of Leeds United. Over the next twenty seasons, almost every Cup Finalist released a single, and some instances had reasonable-sized hits with them. In April 1972, a couple of weeks before their unsuccessful Cup semi-final against Arsenal, Stoke City's fans reached no. 34 in the charts under the name of The Potters, singing a song by Tony Hatch and Jackie Trent, 'We'll Be With You'. Hatch and Trent went on to write the theme song to *Neighbours*, while Stoke went down a few seasons later to the Second Division. In 1973, a group of Spurs fans called themselves The Cockerel Chorus and eased into the top twenty with a tribute to defender Cyril Knowles called 'Nice One Cyril'. Not many Arsenal fans bought that one, though the record's success let everybody know that it was not just the players who could have hits. The fans could, too. By the mid-1990s, well over fifty records dealing with football had charted in Britain, including several by individual soccer stars trying to earn an extra bob or two with their tonsils. Paul Gascoigne's spirited, if unusual, rendition of Lindisfarne's 'Fog on the Tyne' is probably best forgotten. The Spurs duo of Glenn Hoddle and Chris Waddle were well known for their imaginative and creative efforts on the pitch, but they did not allow that reputation to follow them into the recording studio when they made 'Diamond Lights', a no. 12 hit in 1987. A video exists of Terry Venables singing with the Joe Loss Band, but he has not yet recorded anything for commercial release. Kevin Keegan and Ian Wright are forwards who have hit the back of the net many more times, and with greater artistic flair, than the top of the charts, but both have flirted with chart success: Keegan with 'Head Over Heels in Love', a no. 31 hit in 1979, and Wright with 'Do the Right Thing', which peaked at no. 43 in 1993. West Bromwich Albion and England centre forward of the 1960s Jeff Astle was one of the chart-topping England World Cup Squad in 1970, and a quarter of a century later he was proving that his singing success was no fluke by establishing his position as Britain's premier singing footballer with highly individual performances on BBC's weekly *Fantasy Football League* programme. His version of 'Come On Eileen' brings tears to the eyes.

Liverpool's Australian Craig Johnston is the only professional footballer to be credited with writing a top-ten hit, which he did with Liverpool FC's 1988 no. 3 smash 'Anfield Rap (Red Machine in Full Effect)'. One of the performers on this was John Barnes, who probably learned his music from his chairman at Watford, Elton John, who strangely had a hit with a song about tennis ('Philadelphia Freedom' in 1975) but not with one about football – unless you count his 1973 incitement to post-match violence, 'Saturday Night's Alright For Fighting'. John Barnes also took part in the England World Cup Squad's return to the no.1 spot in 1990, 'World in Motion...', giving him two top-three hits and making him at that time the football world's most successful recording star.

However, Liverpool, for all their success on the field and their role in fostering music within the game, never managed a no. 1 hit of their own. It was left to Manchester United to match the England World Cup Squad's achievement of a no. 1 hit. They combined with the eternally youthful Status Quo to create the May 1994 chart-topper, imaginatively titled 'Come On You Reds' (which I suppose could equally apply to Liverpool, or Swindon Town, or Scarborough). This all happened just twenty-four hours after they had beaten Chelsea 4–0 to win the FA Cup, equalling their own record for the biggest winning margin in a Cup Final at Wembley, as well

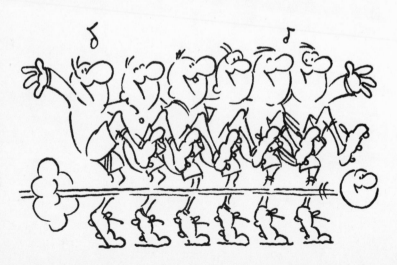

as equalling Tottenham's record of eight FA Cup wins and Arsenal's record twelve Cup Final appearances. They had also matched the record of Preston North End, Aston Villa, Spurs, Arsenal and Liverpool in achieving the Cup and League double, but none of these clubs had also topped the charts. Manchester United's combined sporting and cultural triumph is unprecedented.

The title of Britain's most musical footballer was taken from John Barnes at the same time. Ex-Fulham and QPR defender Paul Parker took over as football's Mr Music. He was the only man to play in both the England squad of 1990 and in Manchester United's 1994 Cup Final team, so this was his second no. 1 hit, a tally equal to such major musical stars as the Bay City Rollers, Culture Club and Jimmy Young. Bryan Robson, another man in whose veins music seems to flow, was captain and vocalist for England in 1990, and he also sang on 'Come On You Reds'. But as he was not officially in Manchester United's Cup Final squad, his performance on the record is rather like Mick Jagger's singing in the background of the Beatles' 'All You Need Is Love' – acknowledged but unofficial.

Britain's least successful club, musically speaking, must surely be Wycombe Wanderers. In 1990–1, they wanted to record a version of Dion's classic hit 'The Wanderer', with words changed to apply more to the Home Counties than the Bronx. They were prevented from doing so by none other than Michael Jackson, whose publishing empire now owns the rights to the song, and who refused to allow a parody to be recorded. At the other end of the scale, the world's most successful musical footballer (excluding Diana Ross, who sang a song and missed a penalty to open the 1994 World Cup) must surely be Julio Iglesias. The Spanish crooner has sold well over 100 million albums, but had it not been for a car accident in the 1960s, when he was a goalkeeper on Real Madrid's books, he might have confined his singing to the post-match bath, and what a loss to the world of popular music that would have been. Less successful, but perhaps more soothing to the ear, was the post-football career of Jack Southworth of Blackburn Rovers and England. Southworth, an FA Cup winner in 1891, scored all four goals in Blackburn's demolition of Derby County when they retained the trophy in 1892, but was forced to retire through injury shortly after these great triumphs. He then became a professional violinist with the Hallé Orchestra.

114

There are a million ways of making money out of football, and most of them have already been tried. It was reported in the national press in March 1996 that sales of Sugar Puffs were plummeting in Sainsbury's in Sunderland. After the initial shock of discovering that: (a) there was something as upmarket as a Sainsbury's in Sunderland, and (b) that a 20 per cent fall in sales in Sugar Puffs in England's newest city was deemed to be a newsworthy event, the reader who persevered with the story would have discovered that the fall in sales was entirely due to a totally inappropriate promotional campaign. The main Sugar Puffs promotional device until then had been a large, hairy and somewhat clumsy creature, possibly modelled on Barry Venison, called Honey Monster, but the marketing men in their wisdom had decided that the time was right for a change in direction. Not only did they put plastic effigies of Premier League footballers in every pack (I could never get my Jamie Redknapp to stand up properly), they also decreed that their new television advertisement should feature Kevin Keegan, the manager of Premiership contenders Newcastle United. This may well have had the right effect on Sugar Puffs sales in many parts of the country, as consumers would have found it just as easy to believe a football manager as a ridiculous furry animal (in many cases, they are one and the same thing), but in Sunderland – then a division lower than their richer rivals along the coast – football allegiances took precedence over taste in breakfast cereal. 'There are people here who will never touch another Sugar Puff in their lives,' said a spokesman for the Sunderland supporters' club, a statement whose significance was somewhat diluted by the fact that there were people dotted all round the country who had already made that decision well before Quaker Oats recruited Kevin Keegan.

Football is big business, and marketing the game is not merely a matter of designing a new Manchester United away kit. The first sponsorship deal was signed in 1980, when John Smith, chairman of Liverpool, announced a shirt-advertising deal with Hitachi. 'We are all desperate for money,' he said, with remarkable honesty, 'and we have got to explore new ways of finding it.' Within a week, Spurs, Everton and Leeds

United had followed suit (or shirt), and had announced clothing sponsorship deals. When Scarborough FC announced a deal with local firm Black Death Vodka, the League was less amused. The idea of Scarborough players roaming the pitches of the lower divisions with a skull and crossbones on their shirts was not deemed to be good for the image of football. Football marketing is also done through items such as World Cup Willie – a mascot, not a disease – which was part of the marketing effort for the 1966 tournament in England. One of the greatest triumphs of marketing that the Arsenal Football Club involved itself in was the renaming of the Gillespie Road tube station from 5 November 1932 as 'Arsenal', and most towns with League clubs realize that the very fact that their name appears on teleprinters and pools coupons every week is good marketing for the town. Some fans might complain that their town is now known as 'Halifax Nil' (or Lincoln Nil, or Chesterfield Nil – I am not trying to make a partisan point here), but at least the town has imprinted itself slightly on the national consciousness, which is what marketing is all about.

But the business does not always work. When Luton Town played Thames, the least successful of all London League clubs, in the Third Division (South) on 6 December 1930, Luton's share of the gate receipts was 1s 7d (about 8p). This amount was paid by postal order, which was never cashed, but was framed and put on display for many years in the Luton Town boardroom. To add insult to injury, Luton lost the game, 1–0, although they took revenge in the return game at Luton, on 11 April 1931, when they won 8–0. And down at Bournemouth they had trouble convincing fans that all was well when a cheque written by the club bounced. It might have been all right, had it been the £210,000 record transfer fee that the club forked out for Gavin Peacock in 1989: most people can understand when a cheque of that size bounces. But it was for rather less than that, for a mere £9, as a refund to a supporter. Bournemouth's chairman claimed it was merely 'a technical matter', but isn't that what all football marketing is?

## EXTRA TIME

*Films about football include*
*Bola Ao Centro* (Portugal, 1947)
*Excuse Me, Are You Watching Football?* (East Germany, 1983)
*Football As Never Before* (West Germany, 1971)
*The Football Parson* (Denmark, 1951)
*Goal!* (UK, 1966)
*A Goal, Another Goal* (USSR, 1973)
*The Goalkeeper's Fear of the Penalty* (Germany, 1971)
*The Klapzuba Football Eleven* (Czechoslovakia, 1938)
*The Last Goal* (Hungary, 1961)
*Let's Go, Wakadaisho* (Japan, 1967)
*When Saturday Comes* (UK, 1996)

*Plays about football include*
*An Evening with Gary Lineker* by Arthur Smith
*Fever Pitch* by Nick Hornby
*The Hammers* by Billy Colvill
*How Steeple Sinderby Won the FA Cup* by J.L. Carr
*Northern Glory* by Phil Woods
*Professional Foul* by Tom Stoppard
*Rattle of a Simple Man* by Charles Dyer
*The Tigers Are Coming OK* by Alan Plater
*Zigger Zagger* by Peter Terson

*Football songs include*
'All I Want for Christmas is a Dukla Prague Away Kit' by Half Man Half Biscuit (1986)
'Ally's Tartan Army' by Andy Cameron (1978)
'Belfast Boy' by Don Fardon (1970)
'Blue is the Colour' by Chelsea FC (1972)
'The Boys in the Old Brighton Blue' by Brighton and Hove Albion FC (1983)
'Daydream Believer (Cheer Up Peter Reid)' by Simply Red and White (1996)
'Diligence and Faith' by Punch and Woking FC (1993)

'Give Them the Old One Two' by Queen's Park Rangers FC (1974)

'Goalie's Ball' by James (1992)

'I'm Forever Blowing Bubbles' by West Ham United Cup Squad (1975)

'I Wish I Could Play Like Charlie George' by The Strikers and Children of Selston Bagthorpe Primary School Choir (1976)

'Leeds Leeds Leeds' by Leeds United FC (1992)

'Manchester United' by Manchester United FC (1976)

'Ole Ola (Mulher Brasiliera)' by Rod Stewart, featuring the Scottish World Cup Football Squad (1978)

118

'Oo Ah Cantona' by Oo La La (1992)

'Ooh Ooh Tony Adams' by the A Team (1995)

'Shouting for The Gunners' by Arsenal FC (1993)

'Three Lions' by Skinner and Baddiel and the Lightning Seeds (1996)

'Viva El Fulham' by Tony Rees and the Cottagers (1975)

'We'll Keep the Blue Flag Flying' by Henry Turtle (1994)

'Wooly Bully' by Vinnie Jones and the Soul Survivors (1994)

'World Cup Willie' by Lonnie Donegan (1966)

*Footballers who have appeared in advertisements include*
John Barnes – Lucozade
Colin Bell – Frosties
Jack Charlton – Shredded Wheat
Brian Clough – Shredded Wheat
Johnny Haynes – Brylcreem
Jimmy Hill – Remington Shavers
Dean Holdsworth – Top Man
Pat Jennings – Unipart
Gary Lineker – Walker's Crisps
David Platt – McDonald's
Trevor Sinclair – Top Man
Ray Wilkins – Tango

*Paul Gascoigne Lookalike Contest*
Held in South Shields, 1990. The winner was a black teenage girl dressed as a fairy.

*Ground opened to public as an ice-rink*
Shay Ground, Halifax, 2 March 1963

# INTERNATIONAL 7
# FAME AND FORTUNE

International football has been with us since 30 November 119
1872, when Scotland and England met on the ground of
the West of Scotland Cricket Club, at Partick. The entire
Scottish team were members of the Queen's Park club, but
rather than wear their club colours of black and white hoops,
Scotland adopted their now familiar dark blue colours. To
identify themselves as British as well as Scottish, they wore
not only blue shirts, but white trousers (they were too long
to be described as 'shorts'), blue and white socks, and red
cowls as headgear. The game ended in a 0–0 draw. At the turn
of the century, Scotland dispensed with their blue jerseys for
just one game, against England in Glasgow on 7 April 1900.

In honour of Lord Rosebery, who had been Prime Minister only four years before, they wore his racing colours of primrose and pink. Far from being laughed off the pitch for daring to turn up in such bizarre outfits, they won 4–1, but never repeated the experiment. On 17 April 1943, the Scottish FA was very short of kit for its wartime international against England at Hampden, and the players were saved from turning out topless only by the intervention of Tommy Walker of Hearts, who had won twenty caps for Scotland between 1935 and 1939. He donated ten of his Scotland jerseys to the players, who showed their appreciation of his generosity by losing 4–0.

Football kit is a sensitive issue. When Manchester United played Southampton at the Dell on 13 April 1996, a crucial game in their attempt to land a third League title in four seasons, they turned out in one of their many alternative strips, this time in grey. At half-time they were 3–0 down, and when they came out for the second half the Red Devils were wearing blue. According to manager Alex Ferguson, this was because the players couldn't see each other in their grey outfits, one of the weaker recorded excuses for being 3–0 down at half-time. The match ended 3–1, so Manchester United could claim that when they could see each other they were the better side, yet in five League games in which they had worn the strip since it had been introduced about a year before, they had gained only one point out of fifteen. United had signed a contract with their strip suppliers that involved them changing their strip at least once every two years, so we can assume that by the turn of the century they will have worked their way through every colour of the rainbow, some with greater luck than others.

Many players and managers, both in Manchester and

beyond, are very superstitious about their team kit, their grounds, their habits and their routines. Jack Tinn, who managed Portsmouth to their only FA Cup win, in 1939, maintained that the spats he wore that year were his club's lucky charm. Burnley once had a china black cat that acted as their lucky mascot, even travelling to away games with the team. A china cat was clearly a better mascot than a real one. When Everton's black cat, which had single-handedly taken them all the way to the FA Cup Final in 1907, fell ill just before the Final itself, their hopes of victory became just as sick. Sheffield Wednesday duly beat them, 2–1. Fulham were presented with a goat as a mascot in the late 1920s, and it did them no good at all. They did not win a single game until they got rid of the goat several months later. (Though whether Fulham's fans noticed this poor run is more debatable: is a losing streak by the Cottagers a curiosity?)

Derby County is a team with which the Fates like to toy, and where superstition seems to play a major role. In 1969, they won promotion as champions of the Second Division, wearing a strip of red shirts and black shorts – the only time in their history that they wore that outfit. Their final game of the season (when promotion was already assured) was away to Millwall, and they brought an all-white strip to wear. Millwall had unfortunately decided on the same strip, so Derby County had to borrow Millwall's change strip, of red shirts and black shorts. Brian Clough was Derby's manager at the time, but when they won the League title for the first time three years later, they did so without once resorting to borrowing Millwall's change strip. Perhaps they should have thought of that option when in 1992–3 they discovered that there was a gypsy curse on their ground. After twelve home games that season, they had won three and lost nine, so they brought in a Skegness clairvoyant (if you are clairvoyant, why would you choose to live in Skegness?) called Adeline Lee to lift the curse. She did this so successfully that of the remaining eleven home games Derby County played that year, they won eight, drew two and lost only one.

Gary Bailey, Manchester United's South African-educated goalkeeper, let in seven goals in his first three Wembley Cup Final appearances. He considered this unlucky, although many people would have considered him extraordinarily lucky to have retained his place in the side, despite letting through so many goals in such important games. After the third of these games, in which United had drawn 2–2 in the 1983 FA Cup Final against Brighton, Bailey decided to take the advice of a South African witch doctor, who told him to tie red and white ribbons to the netting, and attach a padlock as well. Manchester United duly won the replay 4–0, and later in the year they beat Liverpool 2–0 in the Charity Shield. In 1985, on Bailey's last Wembley appearance, Manchester United beat Everton 1–0. Score 7–0 to the witch doctor. By 1990, when Manchester United played Crystal Palace in the FA Cup Final,

Jim Leighton was in goal, minus ribbons and padlocks, and the result was a 3–3 draw. For the replay, less paranormal changes were made. Les Sealey replaced Leighton and United won 1–0.

Four players from Tongogara FC had less luck with witch doctors than Gary Bailey. In an attempt to secure victory in a key game, they consulted their local witch doctor, who advised that to ensure the win they needed, they must urinate on the pitch. All four did so, and all four were banned for life. Despite this minor exception, the black arts seem to serve footballers better than the more conventional white ones. When the new Archbishop of Canterbury, Dr George Carey, and the new Chief Rabbi, Dr Jonathan Sachs, wanted to meet informally to get to know each other, what more religiously neutral site could they choose than Highbury, home of the team they both were reported to support? The date was set for 28 November 1990, the match a Rumbelow's Cup fixture against Manchester United. By all accounts the two religious leaders got on very well, but Arsenal lost 6–2. 'It was a catastrophe,' said Rabbi Sachs after the game. 'We were trying to work out the theological implications. Does it mean our prayers were not heard, that the players were relying on us, or that God is a Manchester United fan?' Given that Manchester United, like Celtic and Liverpool, has always had a strong Catholic tradition, what else could the heads of the Church of England and of the Jewish faith in Britain expect? By the end of the 1995–6 season there seemed little doubt that God, who invented time, was actually on Manchester United's side, as they had managed to score so many vital goals in the heaven-sent minutes added on for injury at the end of almost every game.

We have not been told whether Arsenal ever invited these

123

two religious leaders back to Highbury, seeing how badly they performed in their début match as talismen. Arsenal's most illustrious lucky mascot in the 1930s was Mr W. Crooks, MP, who, like many politicians, liked to be associated with success. It was said that Arsenal never lost when he saw them play, but many suspected that he only told the world whether he had been at Highbury after the game was over and victory had been achieved. The philanthropist Mr Quintin Hogg, founder of the London Polytechnic in Regent Street (now the University of Westminster), played for the Old Etonians in the FA Cup Final, in 1875–6, when they lost 3–0 in a replay to the Wanderers. He had also played in an England v. Scotland game, for Scotland, on 19 November 1870 at Kennington Oval, a match that predates the official series of internationals. Among other players for Scotland in those early games were W.H. Gladstone, son of the great Victorian Prime Minister, and G.G. Kennedy, a cross-country running champion in his spare time.

Politicians have long recognized the importance of identifying with football success. Silvio Berlusconi, briefly Prime Minister of Italy in the 1990s, was also president of AC Milan. Harold Wilson appointed his first Minister for Sport in 1969, choosing Denis Howell, a football referee before he took up the more frivolous pastime of politics. Wilson was never a great sportsman himself but took great pride in the fact that he was Prime Minister on the only occasion that England ever won the World Cup, an event that was to influence his decision-making processes four years later. By 1970, a general election was becoming due, and Wilson, like all his predecessors and successors, was worried about the exact timing. If he were to call the election in June, England would be defending their World Cup title in Mexico at the same time. Defeat for the English team might dent the government's re-election chances. However, when he learned that the matches would only be on television very late at night, Wilson decided to go ahead in June. His reasoning was that football fans, whom he felt were mainly Labour supporters, would not be distracted from their obligation to vote for him by 9 p.m. if the games were not on television until even later than that. His reasoning was, however, faulty. England were beaten by West Germany 3–2 in the quarter-finals on 14 June 1970, and four days later Labour was defeated in the polls. One can only assume that Wilson thought that much of his party's most fervent support lay in Scotland and Wales, where an England defeat would be welcomed as a fine government initiative. England's defeat was less calamitous for their manager, Sir Alf Ramsey, who clung on to office until 1974. When he finally stepped down in the wake of further non-success in the World Cup, an early-day motion in the House of Commons, stating that 'This House wishes to place on record its appreciation of Sir Alf Ramsey for his great services to English football', was signed by six Conservative East Anglian MPs, including Kenneth Clarke, MP, later to become Chancellor of the Exchequer, and Jeffrey Archer, then MP for Louth in Lincolnshire and later to become deputy chairman of the Conservative Party.

In the historic South African elections of 1994 there was a Football Party, whose logo was a football, so that even illiterate voters would easily recognize where to put their X – rather like filling out a pools coupon, really. In England there has been at least one political party whose entire platform concerned football. The Valley Party, which put up several candidates in the council elections in Greenwich in 1990, was solely concerned with ending Charlton Athletic's exile at

Selhurst Park and getting them back to their Valley ground. It received 14,358 votes, which was around 10 per cent of the poll, ahead of both the Liberal Party and Charlton Athletic's average home gate. The party even lived up to its election manifesto promises: the Robins moved to the new Valley Ground in 1992.

King Edward VII, when Prince of Wales, not only played football but attended several major matches. On 20 October 1888, he was present at Kennington Oval to see the Old Carthusians play against the visiting Canadian touring side, the first footballing team from beyond Europe to play in Britain. Prince Alfred of Saxe-Coburg and HRH the Duke of Cambridge were also keen royal followers of football in the Victorian age. King George V, as we have seen, was a keen football fan and his son King George VI, when still merely the Duke of York, not only attended four Wembley Cup Finals as guest of honour but took his wife to see Forfar Athletic play Albion Rovers at Station Park, Forfar, in 1923, when they were staying as guests of the Earl and Countess of Strathmore. That is true devotion to the game. Two of his brothers, the Prince of Wales (afterwards, briefly, Edward VIII) and the Duke of Gloucester, both attended more than one Cup Final, and the Duke of Gloucester was guest of honour at the football League's Jubilee dinner in London on 30 May 1938. Proposing a toast to the Football League, the Duke noted astutely, 'I believe that in the heat of a League contest, partisan feeling among the spectators is sometimes apt to run high, but no one falls out on any more serious subject than a temporary disagreement about the referee's decision.' He was obviously the sort of fan who did not mind who won, as long as it was a good hard game, as was the reporter who wrote, when West Bromwich Albion beat Aston Villa 3–0 on 9 March 1892 to win the FA Cup in the last Final played at Kennington Oval, that West Brom had defeated 'their dear friends and neighbours of Aston Villa'. Such sentiment clearly predates the chant of 'Shit on the Villa', which can be heard around all but one of the grounds of the West Midlands today.

127

Partisan feeling was probably better understood by the Duke of Gloucester's distant cousin, King Carol II of Romania. He came to the throne by the simple means of deposing his own son, King Michael, in 1930. Perhaps in an attempt to win favour with his people, one of his first acts upon ascending the throne was to grant an amnesty to all suspended footballers (suspended because of the bribery and game-fixing that were endemic in Romanian competitive football at the time). He then followed this up by establishing the Romanian Football Association and insisting not only that Romania take part in the first World Cup, due to be played in Uruguay later in the year, but that he pick the team. Nobody disagreed with this regal idea, despite the fact that most European nations did not think it worth travelling all the way across the Atlantic to play in an untried tournament.

King Carol picked the squad, talked personally to their employers to get them time off to play in South America, and then organized the financial support needed to get them there. Once in Uruguay, they performed with some credit, beating Peru 3–1 in their first game. They then went down 4–0 to Uruguay, the ultimate winners of the competition, and were eliminated. In the next two World Cup competitions, in 1934 in Italy and in 1938 in France, Romania took part in the final stages. In 1934, they lost 2–1 to the eventual finalists, Czechoslovakia, despite being 1–0 up at half-time. In 1938, they had much less success. They lost to Cuba, that country's only victory in the World Cup final stages, 2–1 in a replay after a 3–3 draw. Cuba then lost 8–0 to Sweden, which in turn lost 5–1 to Hungary in the semi-finals, which then lost 4–2 to Italy in the final. King Carol II was deposed in 1940 and replaced by his son, an event that owed more to the Second World War than to Romania's declining international football performances.

In 1934, Uruguay, the defending champions, refused to enter the World Cup, partly in retaliation against the European nations that had not bothered to come to Uruguay four years earlier, but also because they were hard pressed to raise any sort of a team. A players' strike was going on in Uruguay at the time, and they remain the only World Cup winners not to defend their title. The Argentinians, who had been runners-up in 1930, sent a team to Italy that included none of the players who had played in that final. The Argentinian FA refused to let any of their top players go to Italy, fearing that they would be poached by the top Italian clubs. This worry was not without substance. Louis Monti, one of the Argentinian finalists in 1930, had already switched sides and played for Italy in their 1934 World Cup-winning side. The

1930 Final, incidentally, was played with an Argentinian ball in the first half (half-time: Uruguay 1, Argentina 2), and with a Uruguayan ball in the second half (full-time: Uruguay 4, Argentina 2).

International football can be a dangerous business, and it is no respecter of rank. Sheikh Mohammed bin Khalid al-Qassimi, a member of Sharjah's royal house, was killed by a firework that exploded in his face as he watched a match between the United Arab Emirates and Egypt on 22 March 1996. Honduras and El Salvador went to war after a bad-tempered World Cup qualifying match, while football in Eastern Europe for almost fifty years after the Second World War was a substitute for war, and scarcely less dangerous, except in the case of fans who turned up to see Kotor play Bokeljan in the Yugoslavian Third Division on 18 August 1990. They discovered the pitch covered with a big-top circus tent. The match was postponed, but fans were allowed in free to watch the circus.

International football competitions are something of a circus these days, except that they make money. When Wrexham, winners of the Welsh FA Cup, were drawn against Manchester United, winners of the English FA Cup, in the second round of the 1990–1 European Cup Winners' Cup competition, they were obliged by UEFA rules to begin their journey to Manchester at least twenty-four hours before the start of the match. As Wrexham to Manchester is a forty-minute coach journey at best, they had to take a very roundabout route to satisfy the European authorities. It did them little good: they still lost 3–0, although their share of the gate money would certainly have covered their travelling expenses. It seems they also made an extra few quid by giving travel advice to Tottenham Hotspur FC. Barely six weeks later, on 1 December 1990, the Spurs team coach taking the first team to play Chelsea stopped at a restaurant for lunch. The coach was parked illegally and the lunch lasted for some time, a combination of events that led first to a parking ticket and then, a little while later, to the coach being clamped. Finally, as the lunch was obviously being strung out, on the advice of Wrexham's travel experts, to fill the entire twenty-four hours that would have been required for the journey, had this been a fixture controlled by UEFA, the coach was towed away, with the team kit inside it. As the Tottenham ground is only a Chris Waddle penalty kick away from Stamford Bridge, they were able to call up spare kit in time for the kick-off and thus avoid the embarrassment of becoming the first League side to play nude. But it has never been explained why Spurs needed to stop for such a long lunch break in a journey of only a few miles. To make their day complete, they then lost the match 3–2.

Two years later, the recondite rulings of the Europeans came into play again, and once more in favour of an English club. When Leeds United played Stuttgart in the UEFA Cup, the aggregate scores were 4–4, but it seemed that Leeds would be eliminated on the 'away goals' rule, Stuttgart having managed one more than Leeds. However, after the match was over, it was claimed that Stuttgart had fielded four foreigners in the second leg at Elland Road, which was one too many for UEFA's liking. So the leg, which Leeds had won 4–1, was awarded to them 3–0, which meant that the teams were now exactly equal and a decider was ordered, in Barcelona of all places. Leeds duly won this game 2–1, but lost to Rangers in the next round. Rangers no doubt began their journey from Glasgow at least twenty-four hours before the kick-off in Yorkshire.

131

The only international match ever played between East Germany and West Germany was at the 1974 World Cup, held in West Germany. The East Germans won 1–0, to finish top of Group One, their goal being scored by Jurgen Sparwasser. Nevertheless, West Germany went on to win the Cup, and a little later Sparwasser defected to the West. When Albania travelled overseas to play France on 30 March 1991, they took a squad of sixteen, an expensive trip for such a poor country. However, such was the patriotic spirit of the footballers that after the game (which they lost 5–0), seven of the team defected to the West, leaving the Albanian authorities only nine return flights to pay for. Libya were not worried about possible defections when they cancelled a World Cup regional match against Algeria due to be played on 20 January 1989. They cancelled it on the grounds that a state of war existed with the United States, which seems spectacularly irrelevant reasoning, even for a football authority. Algeria were awarded the game 2–0, and Libya withdrew from the World Cup.

In football, as in politics, the scoreline is not everything, a fact that Mark Thatcher understands. When his mother became leader of the Conservative Party in 1975, young Mark was asked for his views on this auspicious day for the Thatcher clan. His reply showed a devotion to both football and pan-European feeling that is somehow very moving, as well as almost entirely daft. 'It's like Germany winning the World Cup. It's hard to say why, except that I'm very proud.'

Foreign football, being foreign, is obviously not as good as British football. Was it not Ian Rush who said of his time with Juventus, 'It was like playing in another country'? Luther Blissett failed at AC Milan not because he was not good enough but because, as he said, 'You can't seem to get any Rice Krispies.' After all, the British invented the game and so we must be better than all those foreigners. We play football the way it is meant to be played: we would never allow other considerations to get in the way of the purity of it all. We would not, as Lavrenti Beria did, arrest the president and players of a rival club and send them to prison camps in Siberia. However, Beria was head of the Soviet secret police and had the power to do so, so he did. The president and the Starostin brothers, three of the best players of Moscow Spartak, were all shipped out in 1936 for a very long mid-

season break, so that Moscow Dynamo, the NKVD secret police team, could win a few titles. Moscow Dynamo was founded in 1887 by a pair of English brothers called Charnock, from Blackburn, who went out to Russia to establish a textile factory. That is why Moscow Dynamo play in Blackburn Rovers' colours, blue and white. One cannot imagine John Major imprisoning Alex Ferguson, Eric Cantona and the Neville brothers in order to help Chelsea to the title, but I suppose he would have to do more than nobble Manchester United. By the time he had got Chelsea to a position of football power, he would have imprisoned so many managers and players that the jails would be even fuller than it is Conservative policy to make them.

In fact, it is British policy to let political dissidents play football. Derby County manager Arthur Cox attempted in December 1988 to sign two Czech dissident footballers, Lubos Kubik and Ivo Knoflicek, who had defected from their homeland and were in hiding somewhere in Spain. On 6 January 1989, they were granted political asylum in Britain, but FIFA refused to allow them to play professional football for one year, because they had left the Czech ranks without permission. Despite the fact that Derby County's chairman was the man whose very existence embodied Anglo-Czech co-operation, Robert Maxwell, there is no evidence that the pair ever came out of hiding in Spain, and certainly no evidence that they ever played for Derby County. One can certainly understand why Kubik and Knoflicek were keen to leave Czechoslovakia, as life was obviously very tough there. In 1949, during a glass shortage in Prague, admission to the Prague v. Bratislava League match was five empty bottles.

In Britain, we do not take useful items from spectators as they arrive, we give useful items to them. Cambridge United decided in 1995 to give away condoms at home games, in order to promote awareness of AIDS and safe sex. This did not have the desired effect for all the visitors to the Abbey Stadium; the wife of one Cambridge fan found an unused condom in his coat pocket and assumed that he was having an affair. She promptly walked out on him and refused to return until he managed to show her a story in the local paper confirming his version of events. However, all married men in Cambridge now have a perfect alibi if they are caught playing away on days when Cambridge United play at home.

134

In Britain, we do not have embarrassing technical disasters in pre-season friendlies, but they do in Germany. In a game in August 1995 between Eintracht Braunschweig and Bundesliga runners-up Werder Bremen, the under-pitch water sprinklers came on unexpectedly in the second half, and a fierce jet of water shot high into the air, covering half the pitch. Play was held up for about five minutes, during which time the players cooled off in the spray.

In Britain, we have Vinnie Jones sent off in a Wimbledon *v.* Shanklin, Isle of Wight, pre-season friendly, after an incident in which a Shanklin defender was knocked out, but we do not have embarrassing technical disasters. We save them for the football season proper. Robbie James' 600th League appearance, for Swansea City against Huddersfield on 28 February 1989, had to be abandoned because of a floodlight failure when Huddersfield were leading 1–0. When the game was replayed later in the season, Swansea won 1–0, the scorer being James from the penalty spot. The floodlights failed at Watford in their Fourth Division game against Shrewsbury in the 1958–9 season, and the game had to be abandoned sixteen minutes from the end. Somebody had removed the fuses from the floodlight control box. Watford were fined £100, but were unable to prove who the guilty party was. When the sprinkler system activated itself by mistake towards the end of the Leeds United *v.* Southampton Premiership match on 3 April 1996, it did not stop play, though if it had, it is unlikely that anybody would have cared much. After all, it was only a match upon which Southampton's Premiership survival might have depended, but in Britain we do not try to alter results at the end of a hectic and close-fought season, as is common in lesser territories.

135

At the end of the 1947 season in Belgium, the match between Beerschot and Boom disintegrated into controversy when an aeroplane swooped low over the ground and dropped leaflets onto the pitch. Unfortunately, the plane was so low that the leaflets had not fully separated by the time they hit the ground. Several of them, still falling as one large lump of paper, hit the referee and put him temporarily out of action. While the referee was unsighted in a pile of waste paper, Boom scored. Many referees would have disallowed the goal because of the chaos caused by the surfeit of aerial messages, but in this case, the ref allowed the goal to stand. This did not please

the Beerschot players, who said that the goalscorer was clearly offside but that the ref obviously could not see. The goal stood. In the Romanian Third Division at the end of the 1992–3 season, Viitorul Chirnogeni abandoned a play-off game with twenty minutes to go and only six players still on the pitch. The others had retired ill after having attended a team-mate's wedding party the night before. Chirnogeni were losing 21–0 at the time. In Britain, we are more careful. When Huntly were due to play Burntisland Shipyards in the Scottish Cup on 28 January 1995, Burntisland defender Damien Bray was so confident that bad weather would cause the match to be postponed that he went out for a drink or two with his mates the night before. Unfortunately, the game went ahead, and Bray, after his all-night drinking session and a four-hour coach journey to Huntly, was never likely to be a contender for the Man of the Match award. Huntly won 7–0.

One man who also thought he was an unlikely contender for the Man of the Match award was Fulham's Terry Angus in the Third Division game against Chesterfield in 1995–6. Angus was on the substitutes' bench, and never got onto the pitch, but he still won the supporters' poll for Man of the Match after the 1–1 draw. 'Terry received twenty more votes than anyone else, so we'll have to give him the award,' said a Fulham spokesman. Leicester City's Player of the Season in 1994–5 was their goalkeeper Kevin Poole. When he was presented with his prize, a cut-glass rose bowl, he dropped it and it 'shattered into thousands of tiny pieces'. Poole let through sixty-seven goals in thirty-six League games that year, and Leicester City were relegated.

How Fulham managed to avoid relegation for the first eight seasons of the 1960s will never be known, but perhaps it was the benign influence of Jimmy Hill. On 19 May 1977,

Coventry City, with Hill as managing director, played Bristol City in the final game of the season. Both sides knew that only a win could guarantee survival, but if Sunderland lost at Everton, then both sides would stay up if they drew the game. Stoke City and Spurs were already doomed. The kick-off was delayed, apparently to get all of the 36,903 crowd into the Highfield Road ground, and with five minutes to go, the score was 2–2, with Bristol City pressing forward and looking much the better side. Then the Coventry authorities heard the result from Goodison Park, where Everton had beaten Sunderland 2–0. They flashed the score up on the scoreboard, and all the players knew that provided the match ended in a draw, both teams would retain their First Division status. The match ended 2–2, and Sunderland manager Jimmy Adamson was said to be 'deeply disappointed'.

When Burnley played Stoke in the Test Matches that decided promotion and relegation at the end of the 1897–8 season, both clubs knew that a 0–0 draw would put them both in the top flight for the next year, so that is what happened. Test Matches were abandoned after that, and automatic promotion and relegation instituted. At least those two clubs had an excuse for a 0–0 draw. On 12 December 1931, Newcastle United played Portsmouth in a First Division game. It ended 0–0, and so dull was the game that neither team even gained a corner. The most bizarrely fixed result of all time, though, must be the game between Barbados and Grenada in the National Stadium in Bridgetown, Barbados, in a final group match of the Shell Caribbean Cup in 1993. Barbados needed to beat Grenada by two clear goals to qualify for the finals in Trinidad, and if they failed in this quest, then Grenada would qualify instead. Halfway through the second half, Barbados were leading 2–0 and looked set for the finals. However, a Barbadian defender then scored an own goal and, with the score at 2–1, Barbados looked set to miss out, and Grenada to slip through to Trinidad. Then the Bajans put a little lateral thinking into their interpretation of the tournament rules. In the event of a draw at full time, so the competition organizers decreed, the game would be decided by sudden-death in extra time – the first goal wins. What was more, for some reason that even with hindsight it is hard to understand, any game decided by a sudden-death goal in extra time would be deemed to have been won 2–0, whatever the actual score.

When the full significance of this rule sank in on the Barbados bench, they realized that their only hope of qualifying for the finals was for the score to be drawn at full time, and for them to win in extra time. So the tactics were passed from the bench to the pitch and five minutes of high farce began. In the eighty-seventh minute of normal time, two Barbadian defenders, Stoute and Sealy, turned towards their own goal, exchanged a neat one-two and then Sealy booted the ball into the back of his own net: 2–2 and extra time seemed inevitable. The Grenada players realized they had two options – to score another goal in the final three minutes or, more realistically, to score a goal against themselves and go through to the finals on the basis of losing 3–2. They turned on their own goal, but at this point Sealy showed what a truly remarkable tactical brain he had. Rather than let the Grenada players score an own goal, he martialled the Bajans to stand on the Grenada line to prevent an opposition own goal. The match quickly disintegrated into complete chaos with Barbados trying to prevent a goal at either end, and Grenada being thwarted in their attempts to put the ball past their own keeper. The score at full time was 2–2, and in the fourth

minute of the sudden-death play-off, Thorne scored for Barbados, taking them to Trinidad, because their 3–2 win in extra time counted as 2–0 for calculation purposes.

The Grenada coach, James Clarkson, said, with admirable understatement, 'I feel cheated. The person who came up with these rules must be a candidate for the madhouse. Our players didn't even know which direction to attack. In football, you are supposed to score against the opposition to win, not for them.' Sealy's own goal must be the only one in history to have won the game for his own side.

### EXTRA TIME

*World Cup Final delayed because groundsmen forgot to put corner flags in place*
Munich, West Germany, 7 July 1974

*World Cup Final team scores before the other side touches the ball*
Holland, against West Germany, 7 July 1974. Neeskens scored from the penalty spot in the first minute after Cruyff had been brought down by Vogts before any German player had touched the ball.

*Country qualifies for World Cup Finals by lots drawn by blind Italian boy*
Turkey qualified rather than Spain, in Switzerland, 1954

*World Cup pitch sprayed with sea water and dies*
River Plate Stadium, Argentina, 1978. The pitch had to be relaid.

*Country reaches World Cup Finals after Central Bank unfreezes opponent's assets*
Argentina, needing to beat Peru 4–0 to qualify for the 1978 Finals, chose the week before the game to unfreeze $50 million of Peruvian assets held in Argentina's Central Bank, and also to ship 35,000 tons of free grain to Peru. Argentina won 6–0.

*England captain arrested for stealing jewellery before World Cup*
Bobby Moore, before Mexico Finals, 1970. He was released without charge.

*Woman hangs herself over World Cup result not involving her own country*
A Bangladeshi woman hanged herself when England beat Cameroon in 1990.

*National coach forced to resign for claiming falsely to have played for Notts County*
Jeff Butler, South Africa's coach. His cousin was the one who had played for Notts Co.

*Player jailed for grand larceny for claiming to have scored 17 goals for Stoke City*
Mick Farebrother, 1990. He received $2,000 signing-on fee with San Francisco Blackhawks after telling them he had scored 17 of Stoke's 35 goals the year before.

*Footballer voted Italy's Most Hated Person*
Diego Maradona, in a poll published in December 1990. He beat Saddam Hussein, George Bush and Madonna, among others.

*Footballer sent to Siberia for refusing a transfer*
Eduard Streltsov, Torpedo Moscow, who refused to move to Dynamo Moscow, 1958

*Player's decision not to take part in World Cup prompts 50,000 letters and a song*
Johan Cruyff, Holland, 1978. The song was called 'Oh Johan,

Don't Leave Us In The Lurch'.

*National stadium banned for international matches*
Bolivia's national stadium in La Paz is 3,660 metres above sea level. FIFA's medical committee recommends that no matches are played above 3,000 metres.

*International home matches played overseas*
Faroe Islands home games in European Championships of 1990–1 were played at Landskrona, Sweden, because there was no suitable pitch on the Faroe Islands.

*Player foots bill for national team's travel and accommodation*
George Weah paid for all Liberia's travel and accommodation for qualifying rounds of African Nations Cup, as well as his country's FIFA and Confederation of African Football subscriptions for 1995.

141

# IT ONLY HURTS
# WHEN I THINK
# ABOUT IT

Football can hurt. Ask James Panayi of Watford, who was absolutely ready for his first match for his club in the Avon Insurance Combination League against Swindon on 11 March 1996. However, he did not even last until the opening whistle. He was stretchered off during the pre-match warm-up. The same thing happened to Jim Langley of Fulham, warming up for a match against Arsenal in the early 1960s, when he was laid low by a hefty shot from the unpredictable Tosh Chamberlain, giving the stretcher-bearers some very early work. This sort of tragic event would have come as no surprise to the editors of *The Lancet*, the medical journal, who in the 1860s and 1870s were frequently commenting on accidents on the football field, which proved the intrinsic danger of the sport. When Sir J. Kirkpatrick, Bt, broke his collar-bone while keeping goal for the Wanderers in the Cup Final of 1878, he played on to help his team beat the Royal Engineers 3–1, but the medical press of the day were more scathing of his achievement than the sporting press.

Barney Battles, who played for Celtic and Scotland in the early years of the century, played one complete Scottish Cup tie in 1895 for Dundee against St Mirren with his left arm in a sling. Goalkeeper Sam Hardy of Aston Villa was carried off in the 1913 Cup Final, and his replacement between the posts in those pre-substitute days was the centre half, Harrop, who

was so nervous about using his hands that he routinely headed clear rather than catch the ball. All the same, Villa won 1–0. Terry Butcher played on for England in a World Cup qualifier against Sweden on 6 September 1989 despite having ten stitches put into a head wound at half-time. Garrincha of Brazil played his entire career, which included two World Cup winner's medals, with one leg longer than the other, while Tony Ward, who had his left arm amputated after a motorcycle accident, joined top non-League team Stevenage on 14 September 1990. Ray Daniel of Arsenal played the last part of the 1952 Cup Final with a broken arm, but his team still lost to Newcastle United. Bert Trautmann, the Manchester City goalkeeper, played the final twenty minutes of the 1956 Final with a broken neck. His courage was rewarded, as City ended up winning 3–1.

Sometimes it is hard to tell where the next injury is going to come from, but all a professional footballer can be sure of is that it will come, however hard you try to avoid it. Nick Holmes, the midfielder who was remarkably injury-free as he played over 400 League games for Southampton between 1973 and 1986, went down after a tackle in a match in Barbados on a pre-season tour of the West Indies. He fell on an ants' nest, and was unable to take any further part in the game. Steve Morrow of Arsenal scored the winning goal in the League Cup Final against Sheffield Wednesday at Wembley on 18 April 1993, but broke his right arm in two places in the post-match celebrations, when he was dropped by his Arsenal team-mate Tony Adams. In a pre-season friendly, striker Peter Whitehurst of Grantham Town (President: the Rt Hon. Baroness Thatcher, KG) was involved in an accidental clash of heads with a Norwich City player, and in the process stapled his ear to the side of his head with his earring. Mike Bennett, playing in goal for St Philip's of Bristol in 1989–90, failed to make any attempt to save a shot that whistled past him into the goal. At this point it was discovered that he was suffering from hypothermia. And Chic Brodie, Brentford goalie in the 1960s, was hit by a dog that had run onto the pitch. His injuries virtually ended his career.

Some injuries are less catastrophic, but still cause confusion. Jim Leighton, the veteran Hibernian goalkeeper, was stretchered off the pitch with a split head after a clash with Celtic's John Collins in February 1996 and in his absence Darren Jackson took over in goal. A few minutes later, the ball went out of play and Leighton tried to return to the game, but the referee took a look at his head wound and refused to allow him back on. He signalled for Celtic to resume with a throw-in, but Darren Jackson, who had seen Leighton on the touchline and had assumed he was coming back on the pitch, had gone back to his normal position wearing the no. 10 shirt. The linesmen then flagged to show that Hibs were playing without a goalie, and the referee stopped play as Celtic's

Andreas Thom put the ball into Hibernian's empty net. The goal was disallowed, as the referee claimed that it was against the laws to play without a goalie. Then he allowed Leighton back on. Whether he was right or wrong, it made little difference. Celtic still won 2–1, with Hibernian's consolation goal scored by their erstwhile goalkeeper, Darren Jackson.

Dave Beasant, during his spell at Chelsea, managed to interrupt his career by dropping a bottle of salad cream on his foot. He was out of action for several matches while the injured toe mended. Still, if anybody had tried sucking it as it mended, at least it would have tasted good. When Fulham's goalkeeper Ernest Cromwell Beecham (so named because he was born in Cromwell Road, Hertford) was injured in his side's 0–0 draw against Exeter City on 3 November 1928, there were reports that he had died. It turned out that, although the injury was serious, he was still alive: the confusion had arisen because the Exeter forward at whose feet he had dived to cause the injury was called D'Eath. Beecham was luckier than some. At least two goalkeepers have died as a result of injuries sustained in major games. John Thomson of Celtic was killed in a Rangers *v.* Celtic match at Ibrox Park on 5 September 1931, when he flung himself at the feet of Rangers forward Sam English, and a few years later, Jimmy Thorpe of Sunderland died days after being injured in the game against Chelsea on 1 February 1936. At the inquest, the cause of death was given as diabetes.

Given the physical nature of football, it is surprising that more people have not died while playing, and when David Longhurst of York City collapsed and died shortly before half-time in the game against Lincoln City on 8 September 1990, this was the first fatality during a League game since Sam Wynne died playing for Bury against Sheffield United in 1927.

In April 1948, two players were struck by lightning and killed during the replay of the Army Cup Final, the first game having been played in the presence of King George VI and Queen Elizabeth; and on 25 February 1967, Tony Allden, playing for Shirley in an Amateur Cup Tie, was struck by lightning and died the next day. In May 1969, referee Roy Harper died while in charge of a York *v.* Halifax match. Several devastating injuries have occurred on the football field, some resulting in players wearing odd masks (Paul Gascoigne and Gary Mabbutt) and others in the end of a career (Brian Clough and Derek Dooley, for example). John Thomas of Preston North End broke his leg after only twenty-five seconds of the game against Bolton Wanderers on 18 September 1990, and although Preston still went on to win the game 2–1, Thomas missed the rest of the season, at the end of which he was given a free transfer.

When Fulham played Ashford Town in the first round of the FA Cup on 12 November 1994, in pouring rain on one of the wettest pitches ever used for a major competition match, they came away from the Homelands with what even the most fanatical Fulham fan knew was a lucky draw through two penalties in the last ten minutes. Preparations for the replay at Craven Cottage were not helped by the crop of injuries that followed the first game. Defender Mark Blake was rushed to hospital after the game with burns on his chest, and the next day goalie Jim Stannard and midfielder Micky Adams also complained of burns and blistering. No official cause was ever identified, and none of the Ashford Town players complained of burns, but there was a suspicion that Ashford Town had used pure lime to mark out the lines again at half-time, the first half having been so wet that none of the original markings remained. Obviously, the Fulham players hit the ground rather more than the Ashford players in the second half, which could explain the two penalties. All three were fit for the replay, though, which Fulham won 5–3.

Playing away from home is obviously more dangerous than it looks, which is perhaps why Reg Baines restricted his career to Yorkshire. In the 1930s, when many players found ways to supplement their meagre incomes as professional footballers, Baines had a good job with a chocolate factory in York and thus made sure that whenever he was transferred, he stayed within commuting distance. He played for York City (in two different spells), Sheffield United, Doncaster Rovers, Barnsley and Halifax Town, and never suffered from burns on his chest throughout his career.

Many injuries can be overcome quite easily. Wigan Athletic, then a non-League club, were drawn against Doncaster Rovers in the first round of that year's Cup on 13 November 1965, and they earned a replay thanks to a good goal from their long-serving forward H. Lyon. The game four days later was almost a disaster. Lyon was stretchered off after twenty minutes with torn ligaments in his ankle. This was the first season in which substitutes were allowed, and there was still a reluctance to use them unless the player taken off was obviously never going to walk again. So while Wigan were down to ten men, Lyon spent quarter of an hour in the dressing room, having his ankle strapped, taking painkillers and drinking whisky. He then came back onto the pitch just before half-time, and hobbled gently around on the wing, in the time-honoured fashion of injured forwards. After the interval, during which he may well have swallowed more painkillers and more whisky, he started playing properly. He scored in the fifty-seventh minute, then again in the seventy-second minute, and once more in the eighty-seventh minute. Doncaster Rovers had been beaten 3–1. 'When the first goal went in, I forgot about the pain,' said Lyon. When the hangover hit, he probably forgot about everything.

Some disabilities are not so easily cured. Blackburn Rovers' Norwegian international Lars Bohinen is red/green colourblind, which perhaps means he sees the grass as red, while Manchester United play in green. The problem only affects his play when an orange ball is used, because he cannot see it against a background of green grass and it appears blurred.

In Norway, he is used to playing on snow, which solves the problem. Airdrieonians may have had similar suspicions about their team when the results were not going their way in 1995–6, so they got in an optician to test the team's eyesight. Among those who needed glasses was goalie John Martin. This was not good news, as goalies in glasses are not the most useful variety of the breed. The Preston North End goalie in the 1922 Cup Final is the only one to have worn glasses in FA Cup history. He was J.F. Mitchell, who went on to play once for England in 1925. Preston lost the Cup Final 1–0 to Huddersfield, but at least England did not lose in Mitchell's one international. They drew 0–0 with Northern Ireland in Belfast.

Occasionally injuries occur as a result of interplay with the crowd. This rule applies not only to Eric Cantona at Crystal Palace, but, for example, to Stevie Kirk of Falkirk, in a match against Hearts in the Scottish Premier League. When a teammate went down injured, Kirk kicked the ball into touch so that the physio could come on to treat the injury. Unfortunately, Kirk kicked the ball so hard that it smashed into a twelve-year-old Hearts supporter called Dawn Wilson, who had to be taken to hospital suffering from concussion. The problem did not end there. Hearts fans began pelting Kirk with coins and hamburgers, as well as a rich strain of verbal abuse. Kirk subsequently apologized, but he was not the first player to run foul of the home crowd. When Chelsea toured South America between the wars, in one match their Irish international Sam Irving was hit by an orange thrown from the crowd. Rather than throw it back, Irving peeled it and ate it. Since the 1930s, however, the crowds have got tougher at South American friendlies. A testimonial match for Argentinian striker Mario Kempes, between Rosario Central and Newell's Old Boys, had to be abandoned after seventy minutes after Rosario's Jorge Balbis was knocked cold by a bottle thrown from the crowd.

On 30 October 1886, Preston North End were playing Queen's Park, Glasgow, in the first round of the FA Cup, at Hampden Park, when James Ross of Preston made a strong tackle on W. Harrower, who was injured and could take no further part in the game. There was no chucking of hamburgers, oranges or coins at Ross: the crowd was cannier than that. They waited until the end of the match and then attempted to make their feelings known. Ross and a friend made their escape by running several miles over the surrounding fields. It is possible that the crowd was not merely angry at the injury to their hero, Harrower. Preston North End, which had been disqualified from the FA Cup the previous season for professionalism, had won 3–0 and thus inflicted on Queen's Park – still an amateur side – the only home defeat they ever suffered in the English FA Cup. That seems good enough reason to chase your opponents' leading goalscorer across the countryside for an hour or two.

Nobody was ever charged with any offence after that particular instance of threatening behaviour, but football has often come up against the law, and usually the law has won. Most important cups have been stolen at one time or another, including the Jules Rimet Trophy, which seems to have spent more time in the hands of burglars than in the hands of World Cup-winning captains. And very few investigations of the robberies seem to result in the conviction of the culprit. In 1966, the World Cup was found by the Rotherhithe mongrel Pickles under a hedge in a front garden, after a robbery that was never solved. What is less well known is that Pickles subsequently hanged himself, apparently when his collar got caught in a tree. But was it actually suicide out of remorse, the poor dog being unable to live with the guilt of claiming credit for finding a trophy that he had in fact stolen in the first place? We shall never know.

In 1924, League champions Huddersfield Town discovered that three previous winners of the title (Sunderland in 1913, Blackburn Rovers in 1914 and Everton in 1915) had not bothered to have their names inscribed on the trophy. Huddersfield undertook to remedy the oversight, but as the official League history records, 'The clubs which had not had sufficient interest in even this record of their success were ordered to be debited with the cost.' Maybe lack of interest in the trophies won is the reason why so many of them go missing. The FA Cup was stolen in September 1895, when Aston Villa, the holders, had allowed it to be displayed in the window of Shillcock's boot shop in Newtown Row, Birmingham. It was never recovered, so a second Cup was made, but Aston Villa were fined £25 by the FA for their carelessness. In 1958, an eighty-three-year-old man named Harry Burge confessed to stealing the trophy and melting it down that same night to make counterfeit half crowns. Sixty-three years is the record so far for stealing a football trophy and retaining your freedom, but Peralta, the mastermind behind the theft in 1985 of the Jules Rimet Trophy, managed eight years of freedom. He went on the run in 1986 and was only recaptured in 1994.

In Britain we are obviously better at keeping villains behind bars, which in part explains why, in 1893, Reading became the only team to win a Cup tie with the winning goal scored by an escaped prisoner. Jimmy Stewart, a soldier in the King's Own Regiment based at Aldershot, was under detention for some unrecorded breach of discipline, when Reading needed him to play for them against Southampton St Mary's in the third qualifying round. This was a needle match, because two years earlier the two teams had been drawn against each other at Southampton's Antelope Ground, and Southampton had won 7–0, only to be disqualified by the FA for a breach of the rules. This time, the venue was Reading and club secretary Horace Walker was determined to put out the strongest side possible, which meant that Private Stewart had to play. Walker's plan was simple and effective. He went to the barracks armed with two bottles of Scotch whisky, got Stewart's guards drunk and organized the prisoner's release for the night. Stewart played and even scored the winner in the 2–1 victory over Southampton, then got back into the barracks undetected. However, the story leaked out and when Southampton heard about it, they protested to the FA. However, the committee ruled that there was nothing in the Cup rules about playing escaped prisoners, so the result was allowed to stand. Two rounds later, though, nemesis caught up with Reading. They were drawn against Preston North End and lost 18–0, still the biggest victory by a League club in the FA Cup and beaten only by Preston's 26–0 win over Hyde the year before

the Football League was founded, which of course means that PNE were not a League club at that time.

Prisoners are often good at football. It is not only the likes of Jan Molby, Tony Adams, Duncan Ferguson and Mickey Thomas whose footballing careers were interrupted by a period behind bars. In August 1990, Oxford United sent a scout to watch Paul Reynolds, a prisoner in Aylesbury jail, who was serving a sentence for armed robbery. An inmate at Channings Wood Prison, at Newton Abbot, offered to extend his sentence by one day in June 1986 so that he could play for the prison football team in the Devon Intermediate Final against Wessex Rangers. Ten years later, Channings Wood Prison reached the final again, but when the organizers stated that the final would have to be played on a neutral ground, the Home Office refused permission for the prisoners to leave Channings Wood to play. The only solution was for the prison to be represented by the warders, which they were. The warders lost 16–0.

One of the most lucrative football crimes to commit is to

steal tickets and sell them through the black market. For big games like Cup Finals and local derbies, this can seem to be an easy way to earn a few dishonest pounds. However, Exeter City *v.* Chesterfield is not such a sure-fire route to untold wealth. Thieves who stole 200 tickets from Exeter's ticket office for the upcoming clash with Chesterfield found that they could not sell them on the black market, and they did not even bother to come to the game themselves. Police at the game who tried to catch those who had handled the stolen tickets were disappointed, but perhaps not surprised, that none of the tickets were presented. 'Perhaps that says something about the quality of the game, if no one wanted the tickets,' said a police spokesman.

The thieves were no doubt working on the theory that even the worst teams have some kind of support. Poole Town, whose thirty-eight consecutive defeats at the start of the 1995–6 Beazer Homes League season equalled the record, got their largest crowd of the season, about 500, for the game against Erith and Belvedere, but the conditions were so bad that the referee was forced to abandon the game. The two sides then agreed to play a friendly game, thirty minutes each way, to entertain the crowd, but that ended 0–0 and the crowd went away hardly feeling entertained. Still, Poole can feel that they are not necessarily the worst-supported team in the country. A late challenge for that title was made by Bristol City, which played at Shrewsbury's Gay Meadow in an Auto Windscreens Shield game in 1995–6. Of the total crowd of 2,258, only one man was standing in the Station End, reserved for visiting fans. The PA announced a warm welcome to 'Bristol City and their supporter', and his efforts were so heartening for the Robins that they only lost by the narrowest of margins – seven goals to six in a penalty shootout.

This unnamed supporter would certainly not be put off by travelling long distances to support his team. And when Roy Wright bought a season ticket to new Scottish League club Caledonian Thistle, based in Inverness, he was one of many who thought that Britain's most northerly League team was well worth supporting. He was, however, the only Thistle regular who lived in Brighton. Every weekend, he undertook a 1,200-mile round trip to watch his team. Mike Rowell, a Grimsby fan, decided to get on his bike to watch his favourite club play against West Ham United in the fourth round of the FA Cup in 1996. His 220-mile journey took him through blizzards and snowdrifts, but nothing could stop him from seeing his heroes play. At least, nothing except the weather through which he had pedalled so bravely. When he arrived at Upton Park, he was told that the game was off. 'If only I'd rung to check,' said the exhausted Rowell, 'I could have saved myself all the trouble.' If he'd gone by train, he would have saved himself most of the trouble, but the point of being a football fan is that it is not logical.

The most illogical thing a fan can do is to name his children after his favourite team. The number of children born in 1966 whose first names are Banks Cohen Wilson Charlton Moore Stiles Charlton Ball Hunt Hurst Peters is unrecorded, but at least they bear the names of people who always played for England. Newcastle lads called Cole, Leeds babies called Cantona and Liverpool infants called Beardsley only prove the short-term thinking of their parents, and may well create problems with their allegiances in later life. Joe Park, who lives in Lambton near Newcastle, went one better, and changed his surname to St James Park, so he now has a wife, two sons, two daughters and a grandson, all of whom bear the name of Newcastle's ground. His grandson's full name is

Kieran Gillespie St James Park, so for his sake Newcastle are being urged not to move to a new ground like their near neighbours Middlesbrough.

Football affects the very young, so it is easy enough to understand why Scarborough, in an attempt to boost crowds, established a crèche at the end of the 1990–1 season. It is also obvious why, for example, so many young boys in Blackburn are now being named Alan, but it is less clear why the Under-12 football team at Aleoric School in Melksham, Wiltshire, should consist in 1996 of eleven players and a substitute all called Christopher. Despite the confusion of shouts from the touchline of 'Chris! Pass it to Chris!', they were far more successful than the Beddington Eagles Under-12 team from Sutton, which let through 279 goals in eighteen matches in 1994–5. Perhaps they should have tried to sign Christer McNulty, who was banned by the Scottish FA for ten years for lying about his age, so that he could play for an Under-12 side even though he was already twelve. Obviously, pretending to be eleven when you are really twelve is a far worse crime than head-butting an opponent or making a flying drop-kick into the crowd.

A nineteen-year-old fan was accused of disorderly conduct at the Scottish Cup semi-final between Celtic and Dundee on 7 April 1973. James Burke was arrested during the match at Hampden Park and accused of 'shouting, bawling and screaming'. He was further charged at Glasgow Sheriff Court with assaulting a policeman, but the case against him fell apart when it was revealed that Mr Burke was a deaf-mute. However, being a deaf-mute is not sufficient defence against using abusive language in Staffordshire. Also in 1973, the North Staffordshire Deaf and Dumb team had two players fined £5 each and suspended for six weeks for 'foul and abusive language', and a third fined £5 and suspended indefinitely for abusing and striking the referee.

Football is a passion for all nations and all ages. Mrs Ellen White of Burnage in Manchester received the sort of communication from her local council that many mothers may dread but still half-expect. She was told that she must control her sons, who were persistently playing football in the street, without regard for other people in the neighbourhood. 'Your sons have been identified as some of those involved,' said the council's letter. At the time the letter was written, Mrs White was ninety years old, and her sons were sixty-four, sixty and fifty-nine. A Manchester housing department official later admitted that the letter had gone to the wrong person by mistake, but I wonder? Many of us will still be wanting to play football in our sixties, on the streets, on wasteland, at Wembley Stadium – or anywhere. At least, we can dream.

**INJURY TIME**
*Large hole appears in football pitch*
Crater 5 yards wide and 2 yards deep appeared in Devizes Town (Great Mills Western League) pitch, 1996

*Air travel banned by Football League*
In October 1932, the Football League banned air travel to fulfil
League fixtures, because of insurance problems.

*Fan injured celebrating goal*
QPR season-ticket holder Jonathan Schuman dislocated his
shoulder celebrating Trevor Sinclair's goal in a Coca-Cola Cup tie
*v.* Millwall on 27 October 1993. He was given painkillers by the
club doctor and later needed an operation.

*Fan banned for assaulting referee*
Eighty-two-year-old Sam Phillips banned from attending Ledbury
Town home games in 1980–1 season for allegedly attacking
referee and leaving his shirt 'torn beyond repair'. Mr Phillips
watched Ledbury's remaining home games through a gap in the
hedge.

*Fan banned for kissing referee*
Thirty-year-old Sye Webster banned from Arbroath's Gayfield
Stadium for one year for invading the pitch and kissing the
referee, after Arbroath scored a fifth goal against East
Stirlingshire, 11 March 1995. Mr Webster watched Arbroath's
remaining games from over a school wall by the ground.

*Player shot dead by president of club*
Cassio Barros da Silva, of CSE Palmeira dos Indios, shot dead by
Gilson Raimundo Veija after asking for a transfer, 1995

*Player stabbed by wife*
Alvaro Pena, of Temuco and Bolivia, stabbed by Marie Pena who
was demanding a divorce, 1994

*Poor crowds*
0 – Burton Albion *v.* Leicester City, at Coventry City, FA Cup,
January 1985. The match was a replay behind closed doors after
Burton's goalie had been knocked out by a missile from the crowd
in the original game.
13 – Stockport *v.* Leicester City, 7 May 1921
213 – Hafnarfjordur *v.* Dundee United, European Cup Winners'
Cup, 18 September 1990
409 – Chester City *v.* Bury, Daf Trophy, 27 November 1990
20,470 – Tottenham Hotspur *v.* Sheffield United, FA Cup Final
replay at Bolton, 1901. The lowest Cup Final attendance this

century came about because the railway company was refusing cheap excursion tickets, as Bolton station was being rebuilt.

### Goalposts ripped out by crowd
Wembley Stadium, 4 June 1977, after Scotland beat England 2–1
Goldstone Ground, Brighton, after 18 minutes of Brighton v. York City, 27 April 1996

### Goal destroyed by forward
Reg Culter, Bournemouth v. Wolverhampton Wanderers, 26 January 1957, collided with goalpost in the 6th minute and destroyed the goal. There was a 7-minute delay while the goal was rebuilt, and 35 minutes later Culter scored the only goal of the match.

### Boy comes out of coma after hearing tape of his team's victory
Fifteen-year-old Gareth Knight came out of a 6-week coma after being played a tape of Bolton Wanderers beating Reading 4–3 in the 1995 First Division play-offs at Wembley.

### Club investigated over incentive bonus of overcoat
In January 1948 Fulham director Tommy Trinder offered his overcoat to any player who scored a hat-trick in the FA Cup 4th round tie against Bristol Rovers. Arthur Stevens scored three, and Trinder was seen hanging over the Craven Cottage balcony, waving the coat. The matter was investigated by the FA, who 'suspected an illegal payment may have been made'.

### Unlikely quantity of goals scored in end-of-season game
Hapoel Kiryat, Israeli Division III, beat Hapoel Shtullm 25–0 at end of 1990–1 season. They needed to make up goal difference on promotion rivals.

### FA Cup finalists despite losing a match on the way
Sheffield Wednesday, 1890. In the quarter-finals they met Notts County and won 5–0. Notts County protested, the match was replayed and County won 3–2. Then Wednesday protested and the game was replayed a second time. Sheffield Wednesday won 2–1.
Charlton Athletic, 1946. This season the FA Cup matches were played in two legs as there was no official League programme. Charlton lost 2–1 to Fulham in the second leg of their 3rd round tie, after winning the first leg 3–1.

*Five men collapse exhausted before end of match*
Blackpool *v.* Chelsea, First Division, 29 October 1932. Chelsea
finished with only six men. Blackpool won 4–0.
Manchester City *v.* Woolwich Arsenal, First Division, 1 September
1906. Manchester City finished with six men. Arsenal won 4–1.

*Star player killed by pig*
Mistar, 25, killed by pigs that overran a pitch where Indragiri
Hulu players were practising before an Independence Cup fixture,
Indonesia, 1995